Growing in the Gospel

The Psalms Project Volume Twelve

Discovering the Spiritual World through the Psalms – Psalm 111 - 120

Michael Harvey Koplitz

TABLE OF CONTENTS

The goal of this project:

This research project will examine the 150 psalms for the spiritual awareness each Psalm offers. Each Psalm will be examined by its language and the commentary of the Sages. The spiritual awareness analysis will be done in alignment with Ari's definition of the Tree of life, the Book of Creation, and the Zohar. Each verse of the Psalm will be rewritten using the intent of the language and spiritual commentary to convey its spiritual lesson.

The main resources:

The Zohar

The Book of Creation

Ari's writing on the Tree of Life and the Ten Sefirot

The Theological Wordbook of the Old Testament

Samson Hirsch's commentary on the Psalms

Tehillim – Psalms – A new translation with a commentary anthologized from the Talmudic and rabbinic sources

Accordance Bible Software

Psalm 111

New American Standard 1995	Hebrew

Psa. 111:1 [1]Praise [2]the LORD!
    I [a]will give thanks to the LORD with all *my* heart,
    In the [b]company of the upright and in the assembly.
[2]   [a]Great are the works of the LORD;
    They are [1b]studied by all who delight in them.
[3]   [1a]Splendid and majestic is His work,
    And [b]His righteousness endures forever.
[4]   He has made His [1]wonders [2]to be remembered;
    The LORD is [a]gracious and compassionate.
[5]   He has [a]given [1]food to those who [2]fear Him;
    He will [b]remember His covenant forever.
[6]   He has made known to His people the power of His works,
    In giving them the heritage of the nations.
 	
Psa. 111:7   The works of His hands are [1a]truth and justice;
    All His precepts [b]are [2]sure.
[8]   They are [a]upheld forever and ever;
    They are performed in [1b]truth and uprightness.
[9]   He has sent [a]redemption to His people;
    He has [1]ordained His covenant forever;
	Psa. 111:1 הַלְלוּ יָהּ ׀ אוֹדֶה
	יְהוָה בְּכָל־לֵבָב בְּסוֹד
	יְשָׁרִים וְעֵדָה׃ [2] גְּדֹלִים
	מַעֲשֵׂי יְהוָה דְּרוּשִׁים לְכָל־
	חֶפְצֵיהֶם׃ [3] הוֹד־וְהָדָר
	פָּעֳלוֹ וְצִדְקָתוֹ עֹמֶדֶת לָעַד׃
	[4] זֵכֶר עָשָׂה לְנִפְלְאֹתָיו חַנּוּן
	וְרַחוּם יְהוָה׃ [5] טֶרֶף נָתַן
	לִירֵאָיו יִזְכֹּר לְעוֹלָם
	בְּרִיתוֹ׃ [6] כֹּחַ מַעֲשָׂיו הִגִּיד
	לְעַמּוֹ לָתֵת לָהֶם נַחֲלַת
	גּוֹיִם׃ [7] מַעֲשֵׂי יָדָיו אֱמֶת
	וּמִשְׁפָּט נֶאֱמָנִים כָּל־
	פִּקּוּדָיו׃ [8] סְמוּכִים לָעַד
	לְעוֹלָם עֲשׂוּיִם בֶּאֱמֶת וְיָשָׁר׃
	[9] פְּדוּת ׀ שָׁלַח לְעַמּוֹ צִוָּה־
	לְעוֹלָם בְּרִיתוֹ קָדוֹשׁ וְנוֹרָא
	שְׁמוֹ׃ [10] רֵאשִׁית חָכְמָה ׀
	יִרְאַת יְהוָה שֵׂכֶל טוֹב לְכָל־

<table>
<tr>
<td>

[b]Holy and [2]awesome is His name.
10 The [1a]fear of the LORD is the beginning of wisdom;
A [b]good understanding have all those who [2]do *His commandments;*
His [c]praise endures forever.

</td>
<td>

עֹשֵׂיהֶם תְּהִלָּתוֹ עֹמֶדֶת לָעַד׃

</td>
</tr>
</table>

References

Psalm 111:1
[1]Or *Hallelujah! I will*
[2]Heb *YAH*
[a]Ps 35:18; 138:1
[b]Ps 89:7; 149:1

Psalm 111:2
[1]Lit *sought out*
[a]Ps 92:5
[b]Ps 143:5

Psalm 111:3
[1]Lit *Splendor and majesty*
[a]Ps 96:6; 145:5
[b]Ps 112:3, 9; 119:142

Psalm 111:4
[1]I.e. wonderful acts
[2]Lit *a memorial*
[a]Ps 86:5, 15; 103:8; 145:8

Psalm 111:5
[1]Lit *prey*
[2]Or *revere*
[a]Matt 6:31-33
[b]Ps 105:8

Psalm 111:7
[1]Or *faithfulness*
[2]Or *trustworthy*
[a]Rev 15:3
[b]Ps 19:7; 93:5

Psalm 111:8
[1]Or *faithfulness*
[a]Ps 119:160; Is 40:8; Matt 5:18
[b]Ps 19:9

Psalm 111:9
[1]Lit *commanded*
[2]I.e. inspiring reverence
[a]Luke 1:68
[b]Ps 99:3; Luke 1:49

Psalm 111:10
[1]Or *reverence for*
[2]Lit *do* them
[a]Job 28:28; Prov 1:7; 9:10; Eccl 12:13
[b]Ps 119:98; Prov 3:4
[c]Ps 145:2

Targum

Psa. 111:1 Hallelujah! I will sing praise in the presence of the LORD with all my heart in the secret of the upright and the assembly. **2** The deeds of the LORD are great; they are sought for by all who desire them. **3** His work is praise and glory, and his merit endures for ever. **4** He made a good memorial for his wonders; the LORD is gracious and merciful. **5** He gave food to those who fear him; he will remember his covenant forever. **6** The might of his deeds he told to his people, to give them the inheritance of the Gentiles. **7** The works of his hands are truth and justice; all his commands are faithful. **8** They are reliable for ever and ever; they are done in truth and uprightness. **9** He sent redemption to his people; he commanded his covenant for ever; his name is holy and awesome. **10** The beginning of wisdom is fear of the LORD, good understanding to all who do them; his praise endures forever.

Spiritual Awareness

Introduction

The Sage Sforno said this Psalm is a sermon exhorting the ordinary Jew to devote time to Torah study. The uneducated person usually uses one of the following reasons for not studying the Torah: it is too difficult, or their livelihood takes up all their time. The Psalmist responds to these excuses by telling the people that they need to be indebted to the LORD for the kindness from the Sefirah Chesed. The best way to thank the LORD is to study Torah. The beginning of wisdom is a reverence for the LORD. This is done through the execution of the mitzvot in the Torah.

Notes on the Psalm

The English versions like to say "fear of the LORD." The translation "reverence" is preferable in a spiritual awareness sense. The idea of fear says that the LORD will take vengeance on His people if they do not follow him. Jewish parents use the fear of the LORD to scold their children. The adult becomes fearful of the LORD's retribution when this is done. This attitude tends to drive adults away from the LORD. It is not pleasant to imagine an angry God watching every move a person makes.

It is better to show reverence. This Psalm says that a person demonstrates reverence to the LORD by following the Torah and performing the mitzvot. The LORD created everything in the Universe. The LORD deserves reverence and gratitude.

Psalm 112

New American Standard 1995	Hebrew
Psa. 112:1 [1]Praise [2]the LORD! How [a]blessed is the man who [3]fears the LORD, Who greatly [b]delights in His commandments. 2 His [1a]descendants will be mighty [2]on earth; The generation of the [b]upright will be blessed. 3 [a]Wealth and riches are in his house, And his righteousness endures forever. 4 Light arises in the darkness [a]for the upright; *He is* [b]gracious and compassionate and righteous. 5 It is well with the man who [a]is gracious and lends; He will [1]maintain his cause in judgment. 6 For he will [a]never be shaken; The [b]righteous will be [1]remembered forever. **Psa. 112:7** He will not fear [a]evil tidings; His [b]heart is steadfast, [c]trusting in the LORD. 8 His [a]heart is upheld, he [b]will not fear, Until he [1]looks *with satisfaction* on his adversaries. 9 [1]He [a]has given freely to the poor, His righteousness endures forever; His [b]horn will be exalted in honor.	הַלְלוּ יָהּ ׀ אַשְׁרֵי־אִישׁ **Psa. 112:1** יָרֵא אֶת־יְהוָה בְּמִצְוֹתָיו חָפֵץ מְאֹד ׃ 2 גִּבּוֹר בָּאָרֶץ יִהְיֶה זַרְעוֹ דּוֹר יְשָׁרִים יְבֹרָךְ ׃ 3 הוֹן־וָעֹשֶׁר בְּבֵיתוֹ וְצִדְקָתוֹ עֹמֶדֶת לָעַד ׃ 4 זָרַח בַּחֹשֶׁךְ אוֹר לַיְשָׁרִים חַנּוּן וְרַחוּם וְצַדִּיק ׃ 5 טוֹב־אִישׁ חוֹנֵן וּמַלְוֶה יְכַלְכֵּל דְּבָרָיו בְּמִשְׁפָּט ׃ 6 כִּי־לְעוֹלָם לֹא־ יִמּוֹט לְזֵכֶר עוֹלָם יִהְיֶה צַדִּיק ׃ 7 מִשְּׁמוּעָה רָעָה לֹא יִירָא נָכוֹן לִבּוֹ בָּטֻחַ בַּיהוָה ׃ 8 סָמוּךְ לִבּוֹ לֹא יִירָא עַד אֲשֶׁר־יִרְאֶה בְצָרָיו ׃ 9 פִּזַּר ׀ נָתַן לָאֶבְיוֹנִים צִדְקָתוֹ עֹמֶדֶת לָעַד קַרְנוֹ תָּרוּם בְּכָבוֹד ׃ 10 רָשָׁע יִרְאֶה ׀ וְכָעָס שִׁנָּיו יַחֲרֹק וְנָמָס תַּאֲוַת רְשָׁעִים תֹּאבֵד ׃

Psa. 112:10 The [a]wicked will see it and be [1]vexed,
 	
    He will [b]gnash his teeth and [c]melt away;
 	
    The [d]desire of the wicked will perish.	

References

Psalm 112:1
[1]Or *Hallelujah! Blessed*
[2]Heb *YAH*
[3]Or *reveres*
[a]Ps 128:1
[b]Ps 1:2; 119:14, 16

Psalm 112:2
[1]Lit *seed*
[2]Or *in the land*
[a]Ps 102:28; 127:4
[b]Ps 128:4

Psalm 112:3
[a]Prov 3:16; 8:18; Matt 6:33

Psalm 112:4
[a]Job 11:17; Ps 97:11
[b]Ps 37:26

Psalm 112:5
[1]Or *conduct his affairs with justice*
[a]Ps 37:21

Psalm 112:6
[1]Lit *for an eternal remembrance*
[a]Ps 15:5; 55:22
[b]Prov 10:7

Psalm 112:7
[a]Prov 1:33
[b]Ps 57:7; 108:1
[c]Ps 56:4

Psalm 112:8
[a]Heb 13:9
[b]Ps 27:1; 56:11; Prov 1:33; 3:24; Is 12:2
[c]Ps 54:7; 59:10

Psalm 112:9
[1]Lit *He has scattered, he has given to...*
[a]2 Cor 9:9
[b]Ps 75:10; 89:17; 92:10; 148:14

Psalm 112:10
[1]Or *angry*
[a]Ps 86:17
[b]Ps 35:16; 37:12; Matt 8:12; 25:30; Luke 13:28
[c]Ps 58:7
[d]Job 8:13; Prov 10:28; 11:7

Targum

Psa. 112:1 Hallelujah! Happy is the man who fears the LORD; he takes great pleasure in his commandments. ² His children will be mighty in the Torah, he will be blessed in the generation of the upright. ³ Luck and riches are in his house, and his merit endures forever. ⁴ Light dawns in darkness for the upright, gracious, and merciful, and righteous. ⁵ A good man pities the poor and lends money; he will support his words according to rule. ⁶ For he will never be moved; the righteous man is [destined] for eternal memory. ⁷ He will not fear news of disaster; his heart is firm, trusting in the word of the LORD. ⁸ His heart is steady, he will not be afraid, until he sees redemption in distress. ⁹ He scattered his wealth, gave it to the needy; his merit endures forever, his might will rise up in glory. ¹⁰ The wicked man will see and be angry, he will grind his teeth at him and rot; the desire of the wicked will perish.

Spiritual Awareness

Introduction

This Psalm is a continuation of Psalm 111. Praiseworthy is the person who reveres the LORD.

Verse three

The idea that a person who reveres the LORD will instantly have material wealth and riches is to misunderstand this verse. The English versions use the translation "fear" instead of "reverence." It is important to revere the LORD as the creator of Heaven and Earth. When one is respectful to the LORD, one follows the ways of the Torah. Thus, the person will perform the mitzvot of the Torah. The wealth and riches described in this verse are spiritual riches. This enables the person to store treasures in Heaven. When judgment day arrives, the person will be ahead in spiritual wealth, and the LORD will view the person as a tzaddik.

Spiritual wealth and riches come into his house, and his righteousness shall endure forever.

Notes on the Psalm

The remainder of the Psalm, except the last line, describes what it means to be tzaddik (a righteous person) in the eyes of the LORD. The last line says that the lawless person will be jealous of the tzaddik because an evil person will not have spiritual treasures on Earth or in Heaven.

Psalm 113

New American Standard 1995	Hebrew
Psa. 113:1 [1]Praise [2]the LORD! [a]Praise, O [b]servants of the LORD, Praise the name of the LORD. 2 [a]Blessed be the name of the LORD From this time forth and forever. 3 [a]From the rising of the sun to its setting The [b]name of the LORD is to be praised. 4 The LORD is [a]high above all nations; His [b]glory is above the heavens. **Psa. 113:5** [a]Who is like the LORD our God, Who [b]is enthroned on high, 6 Who [1a]humbles Himself to behold *The things that are* in heaven and in the earth? 7 He [a]raises the poor from the dust And lifts the needy from the ash heap, 8 To make *them* [a]sit with [1]princes, With the [1]princes of His people. 9 He [a]makes the barren woman abide in the house *As* a joyful mother of children. [1]Praise [2]the LORD!	הַלְלוּ יָהּ ׀ הַלְלוּ עַבְדֵי יְהוָה הַלְלוּ אֶת־שֵׁם יְהוָה׃ 2 יְהִי שֵׁם יְהוָה מְבֹרָךְ מֵעַתָּה וְעַד־עוֹלָם׃ 3 מִמִּזְרַח־שֶׁמֶשׁ עַד־מְבוֹאוֹ מְהֻלָּל שֵׁם יְהוָה׃ 4 רָם עַל־כָּל־גּוֹיִם ׀ יְהוָה עַל הַשָּׁמַיִם כְּבוֹדוֹ׃ 5 מִי כַּיהוָה אֱלֹהֵינוּ הַמַּגְבִּיהִי לָשָׁבֶת׃ 6 הַמַּשְׁפִּילִי לִרְאוֹת בַּשָּׁמַיִם וּבָאָרֶץ׃ 7 מְקִימִי מֵעָפָר דָּל מֵאַשְׁפֹּת יָרִים אֶבְיוֹן׃ 8 לְהוֹשִׁיבִי עִם־נְדִיבִים עִם נְדִיבֵי עַמּוֹ׃ 9 מוֹשִׁיבִי ׀ עֲקֶרֶת הַבַּיִת אֵם־הַבָּנִים שְׂמֵחָה הַלְלוּ־יָהּ׃

References

Psalm 113:1
[1]Or *Hallelujah! Praise*
[2]Heb *YAH*
[a]Ps 135:1
[b]Ps 34:22; 69:36; 79:10; 90:13

Psalm 113:2
[a]Ps 145:21; Dan 2:20

Psalm 113:3
[a]Ps 50:1; Is 59:19; Mal 1:11
[b]Ps 18:3; 48:1, 10

Psalm 113:4
[a]Ps 97:9; 99:2
[b]Ps 8:1; 57:11; 148:13

Psalm 113:5
[a]Ex 15:11; Ps 35:10; 89:6
[b]Ps 103:19

Psalm 113:6
[1]Or *looks far below in the heavens and on the earth?*
[a]Ps 11:4; 138:6; Is 57:15

Psalm 113:7
[a]1 Sam 2:8; Ps 107:41

Psalm 113:8
[1]Or *nobles*
[a]Job 36:7

Psalm 113:9
[1]Or *Hallelujah!*
[2]Heb *YAH*
[a]1 Sam 2:5; Ps 68:6; Is 54:1

Targum

Psa. 113:1 Hallelujah! Give praise, O servants of the LORD, praise the name of the LORD. ² May the name of the LORD be blessed, from now and forever. ³ From the rising of the sun to its setting, the name of the LORD is praised. ⁴ The LORD is high above all Gentiles, his glory is over the heavens. ⁵ Who is like the LORD, our God, whose dwelling is lofty in situation? ⁶ Who lowers his eyes to look on the heavens and the earth. ⁷ Who raises up the poor man from the dust; he will lift up the needy from the ash-heap. ⁸ To make him dwell with the leaders, with the leaders of his people. ⁹ Who makes dwell the congregation of Israel, who is likened to a barren woman who sits beholding the men of her house, full of people, like a mother who rejoices over her sons.

Spiritual Awareness

Introduction

Psalms 113-118 are a series called the "Hallel." These are uplifting Psalms for the Jewish nation. They have sung these Psalms for millennia as the people wandered around the world. These Psalms have kept the people alive during days of trial.

Notes on the Psalm

The name of the LORD is to be praised. Even though today the actual pronunciation of the name is unknown, it is still praised. The name of the LORD was uttered by the High Priest in the Holy of Holies in the Temple at Jerusalem. It was said once a year on Yom Kippur at 3:00 PM when the sacrifice for the forgiveness of the people was made. When the Temple was destroyed the High Priest determined that there was no way to share the name. Therefore, the pronunciation was not passed onto the next High Priest. When the name of the LORD is encountered, the people say the word Adonai. The utterance of the name was forbidden. There is a story in the Torah about two of Aaron's sons dying because they uttered the name of the LORD when they were outside the Holy of Holies in the Tabernacle in the desert.

Psalm 114

New American Standard 1995	Hebrew

Psa. 114:1   When Israel went forth [a]from Egypt,
       The house of Jacob from a people of [b]strange language,
2   Judah became [a]His sanctuary,
       Israel, [b]His dominion.
 	
Psa. 114:3   The [a]sea looked and fled;
       The [b]Jordan turned back.
4   The mountains [a]skipped like rams,
       The hills, like lambs.
5   What [a]ails you, O sea, that you flee?
       O Jordan, that you turn back?
6   O mountains, that you skip like rams?
       O hills, like lambs?
 	
Psa. 114:7   [a]Tremble, O earth, before the Lord,
       Before the God of Jacob,
8   Who [a]turned the rock into a [b]pool of water,
       The [c]flint into a fountain of water.
	בְּצֵאת יִשְׂרָאֵל מִמִּצְרָיִם **Psa. 114:1**
	בֵּית יַעֲקֹב מֵעַם לֹעֵז׃ 2 הָיְתָה
	יְהוּדָה לְקָדְשׁוֹ יִשְׂרָאֵל
	מַמְשְׁלוֹתָיו׃ 3 הַיָּם רָאָה וַיָּנֹס
	הַיַּרְדֵּן יִסֹּב לְאָחוֹר׃ 4 הֶהָרִים
	רָקְדוּ כְאֵילִים גְּבָעוֹת כִּבְנֵי־צֹאן׃ 5
	מַה־לְּךָ הַיָּם כִּי תָנוּס הַיַּרְדֵּן תִּסֹּב
	לְאָחוֹר׃ 6 הֶהָרִים תִּרְקְדוּ כְאֵילִים
	גְּבָעוֹת כִּבְנֵי־צֹאן׃ 7 מִלִּפְנֵי אָדוֹן
	חוּלִי אָרֶץ מִלִּפְנֵי אֱלוֹהַּ יַעֲקֹב׃ 8
	הַהֹפְכִי הַצּוּר אֲגַם־מָיִם חַלָּמִישׁ
	לְמַעְיְנוֹ־מָיִם׃

References

Psalm 114:1
[a]Ex 12:51; 13:3
[b]Ps 81:5

Psalm 114:2
[a]Ex 15:17; 29:45, 46; Ps 78:68, 69
[b]Ex 19:6

Psalm 114:3
[a]Ex 14:21; Ps 77:16
[b]Josh 3:13, 16

Psalm 114:4
[a]Ex 19:18; Judg 5:5; Ps 18:7; 29:6; Hab 3:6

Psalm 114:5
[a]Hab 3:8

Psalm 114:7
[a]Ps 96:9

Psalm 114:8
[a]Ex 17:6; Num 20:11; Ps 78:15; 105:41
[b]Ps 107:35
[c]Deut 8:15

Targum

Psa. 114:1 When Israel came out of Egypt, the house of Jacob from barbarian peoples – **2** The company of the house of Judah became property of his Holy One, Israel of his rulers. **3** When the word of the LORD was revealed at the sea, the sea looked and retreated; the Jordan turned around. **4** When the Torah was given to his people, the mountains leapt like rams, the hills like offspring of the flock. **5** God said, "What is the matter, O sea, for you are retreating? O Jordan, that you are turning around?" **6** O mountains, leaping about like rams? O hills, like offspring of the flock? **7** In the presence of the lord, dance, O earth, in the presence of the God of Jacob. **8** Who turns the flint into a channel of water, the adamant to springs of water.

Spiritual Awareness

Introduction

This Psalm continues the praises of the LORD. Israel became noble when they left Egypt and had faith in the LORD when they were told to enter the Red Sea. The ultimate disciple of the people occurred at Sinai when they accepted the LORD's Torah and the burdens that it brings.

Verse two

The tribe of Yehudah (Judah) represented the concept of might and became the Sanctuary of God. This occurred when the Israelites left Egypt. Yehuda became God's own tribe and sacred to Him. This would explain why the Temple was built in Jerusalem, which was 90% in the tribe's territory.

Yehudah became His Sanctuary, Yisrael His spheres of dominion.

Psalm 115

New American Standard 1995	Hebrew
Psa. 115:1 [a]Not to us, O LORD, not to us, But [b]to Your name give glory Because of Your lovingkindness, because of Your [1]truth. **2** [a]Why should the nations say, "[b]Where, now, is their God?" **3** But our [a]God is in the heavens; He [b]does whatever He pleases. **4** Their [a]idols are silver and gold, The [b]work of man's hands. **5** They have mouths, but they [a]cannot speak; They have eyes, but they cannot see; **6** They have ears, but they cannot hear; They have noses, but they cannot smell; **7** [1]They have hands, but they cannot feel; [2]They have feet, but they cannot walk; They cannot make a sound with their throat. **8** [a]Those who make them [1]will become like them, Everyone who trusts in them. **Psa. 115:9** O [a]Israel, [b]trust in the LORD; He is their [c]help and their shield. **10** O house of [a]Aaron, trust in the LORD; He is their help and their shield.	**Psa. 115:1** ‏לֹא־כִּי לָנוּ לֹא יְהֹוָה לָנוּ לֹא ‏עַל־חַסְדְּךָ עַל־כָּבוֹד תֵּן לְשִׁמְךָ ‏אַיֵּה הַגּוֹיִם יֹאמְרוּ לָמָּה 2 ‏אֲמִתֶּךָ ‏בַשָּׁמַיִם וֵאלֹהֵינוּ 3 ‏אֱלֹהֵיהֶם נָא ‏עֲצַבֵּיהֶם 4 ‏עָשָׂה חָפֵץ אֲשֶׁר־כֹּל ‏פֶּה־ 5 ‏אָדָם יְדֵי מַעֲשֵׂה וְזָהָב כֶּסֶף ‏וְלֹא לָהֶם עֵינַיִם יְדַבֵּרוּ וְלֹא לָהֶם ‏יִשְׁמָעוּ וְלֹא לָהֶם אָזְנַיִם 6 ‏יִרְאוּ ‏יְדֵיהֶם 7 ‏יְרִיחוּן וְלֹא לָהֶם אַף ‏יְהַלֵּכוּ וְלֹא רַגְלֵיהֶם יְמִישׁוּן וְלֹא ‏יִהְיוּ כְמוֹהֶם 8 ‏בִּגְרוֹנָם יֶהְגּוּ־לֹא ‏בָּהֶם 9 ‏בָּטֵחַ אֲשֶׁר־כֹּל עֹשֵׂיהֶם ‏וּמָגִנָּם עֶזְרָם בַיהֹוָה בָּטַח יִשְׂרָאֵל ‏בַיהֹוָה בִּטְחוּ אַהֲרֹן בֵּית 10 ‏הוּא ‏יְהֹוָה יִרְאֵי 11 ‏הוּא וּמָגִנָּם עֶזְרָם ‏הוּא וּמָגִנָּם עֶזְרָם בַיהֹוָה בִּטְחוּ ‏בֵּית־אֶת יְבָרֵךְ זְכָרָנוּ יְהֹוָה 12 ‏אַהֲרֹן בֵּית־אֶת יְבָרֵךְ 13 ‏יִשְׂרָאֵל ‏עִם הַקְּטַנִּים יְהֹוָה יִרְאֵי יְבָרֵךְ ‏עֲלֵיכֶם יְהֹוָה יֹסֵף 14 ‏הַגְּדֹלִים ‏בְּרוּכִים 15 ‏בְּנֵיכֶם וְעַל־עֲלֵיכֶם ‏וָאָרֶץ שָׁמַיִם עֹשֵׂה לַיהֹוָה אַתֶּם ‏נָתַן וְהָאָרֶץ לַיהֹוָה שָׁמַיִם הַשָּׁמַיִם ‏יְהַלְלוּ הַמֵּתִים לֹא 17 ‏אָדָם־לִבְנֵי

11 You who [1][a]fear the LORD, trust in the LORD;
He is their help and their shield.
12 The LORD [a]has been mindful of us; He will bless *us;*
He will bless the house of Israel;
He will bless the house of Aaron.
13 He will [a]bless those who [1]fear the LORD,
[b]The small together with the great.
14 May the LORD [a]give you increase,
You and your children.
15 May you be blessed of the LORD,
[a]Maker of heaven and earth.

Psa. 115:16 The heavens are [a]the heavens of the LORD,
But [b]the earth He has given to the sons of men.
17 The [a]dead do not praise [1]the LORD,
Nor *do* any who go down into [b]silence;
18 But as for us, we will [a]bless [1]the LORD
From this time forth and forever.
[2]Praise [1]the LORD!

יָהּ וְלֹא כָּל־יֹרְדֵי דוּמָה ׃ 18 וַאֲנַחְנוּ
וּ נְבָרֵךְ יָהּ מֵעַתָּה וְעַד־עוֹלָם
הַלְלוּ־יָהּ ׃

References

Psalm 115:1
[1]Or *faithfulness*
[a]Is 48:11; Ezek 36:22
[b]Ps 29:2; 96:8

Psalm 115:2
[a]Ps 79:10
[b]Ps 42:3, 10

Psalm 115:3
[a]Ps 103:19
[b]Ps 135:6; Dan 4:35

Psalm 115:4
[a]Ps 115:4-8; 135:15-18; Jer 10:4
[b]Deut 4:28; 2 Kin 19:18; Is 37:19; 44:10, 20; Jer 10:3

Psalm 115:5
[a]Jer 10:5

Psalm 115:7
[1]Lit *Their hands*
[2]Lit *Their feet*

Psalm 115:8
[1]Or *are like them*
[a]Ps 135:18; Is 44:9-11

Psalm 115:9
[a]Ps 118:2; 135:19
[b]Ps 37:3; 62:8
[c]Ps 33:20

Psalm 115:10
[a]Ps 118:3; 135:19

Psalm 115:11
[1]Or *revere*

[a]Ps 22:23; 103:11; 135:20

Psalm 115:12
[a]Ps 98:3

Psalm 115:13
[1]Or *revere*
[a]Ps 103:11; 112:1; 128:1
[b]Rev 11:18; 19:5

Psalm 115:14
[a]Deut 1:11

Psalm 115:15
[a]Gen 1:1; Neh 9:6; Ps 96:5; 102:25; 121:2; 124:8; 134:3; 146:6; Acts 14:15; Rev 14:7

Psalm 115:16
[a]Ps 89:11
[b]Ps 8:6

Psalm 115:17
[1]Heb *YAH*
[a]Ps 6:5; 88:10-12; Is 38:18
[b]Ps 31:17

Psalm 115:18
[1]Heb *YAH*
[2]Or *Hallelujah!*
[a]Ps 113:2; Dan 2:20

Targum

Psa. 115:1 Not on our account, O LORD, not on account of our merits, but rather to your name give glory, because of your goodness and because of your truth. ² Why will the Gentiles say, "Where now is their God?" ³ And our God's residence is in heaven, all that he desires he has done. ⁴ Their idols are of silver and gold, the handiwork of a son of man. ⁵ They have a mouth, but do not speak; they have eyes, and do not see. ⁶ They have ears, and do not hear; they have nostrils, but do not smell. ⁷ Hands, but do not feel; feet, but do not walk; they do not murmur with their throat. ⁸ May their makers become like them, everyone who relies upon them. ⁹ O Israel, trust in the word of the LORD; he is their helper and their shield. ¹⁰ Those of the house of Aaron, trust in the word of the LORD; he is their helper and their shield. ¹¹ You who fear the LORD, trust in the word of the LORD; he is their helper and their shield. ¹² The word of the LORD has remembered us for good, he will bless; he will bless the house of Israel, he will bless the house of Aaron. ¹³ He will bless those who fear the LORD, the small with the great. ¹⁴ The word of the LORD will add to you; to you, and to your sons. ¹⁵ Blessed are you in the presence of the LORD, maker of heaven and earth. ¹⁶ The heavens of the heavens are for the glorious presence of the LORD, and the earth he has given to the sons of men. ¹⁷ The dead do not praise the name of the LORD, nor any of those who go down to the grave of earth. ¹⁸ But we will bless Yah, from now and forevermore. Hallelujah!

Spiritual Awareness

Introduction

This Psalm speaks to the long-term effects of the LORD's miracles on the Red Sea and Mount Sinai. These events left an indelible mark of faith on the Jewish people that will last until the end of time. The Gentiles of these events were impressed with the LORD but overtime they forgot about these events. The LORD seems to have left human events to unfold by themselves. The Jewish people beseech the LORD to intervene again not only for Yisrael's sake but also for the LORD's name. The Gentiles need to see something from the LORD which will convince them to worship the LORD and to hold Yisrael as sacred.

Verse one

The people call for the loving-kindness of the Sefirah Chesed which will show to the Gentile nations that the LORD is watching events on Earth and will react.

Not to us, O LORD, not to us, but to Your Name give honor, send the loving-kindness from the Sefirah Chesed which demonstrates Your truth.

Verse ten

Yisrael is called to have trust and faith in the LORD. The House of Aaron were the priests. The priests were the people who interpreted Scripture and led the people in worship to the LORD. Therefore, it was imperative from the priests to have the "strongest" faith in the LORD.

O House of Aharon, trust in the LORD for He is their held and their shield.

Notes on the Psalm

The Psalmist says that even though it is difficult to be a Jew, it is imperative to maintain faith and trust in the LORD. It is difficult to trust the LORD when the persecutions from the Gentile nations occur. The Jews are scattered in various countries around the globe. In many countries, they are persecuted for their religious beliefs. The Torah can be a burden, but the rewards will be there. The rewards may not be seen in this life, but certainly will be shown in the world to come.

Psalm 116

New American Standard 1995	Hebrew

Psa. 116:1 ᵃI love the LORD, because He ᵇhears
　　My voice *and* my supplications.
2　　Because He has ᵃinclined His ear to me,
　　Therefore I shall call *upon Him* as long as I live.
3　　The ᵃcords of death encompassed me
　　And the ¹terrors of ²Sheol ³came upon me;
　　I found distress and sorrow.
4　　Then ᵃI called upon the name of the LORD:
　　"O LORD, I beseech You, ¹ᵇsave my life!"

Psa. 116:5 ᵃGracious is the LORD, and ᵇrighteous;
　　Yes, our God is ᶜcompassionate.
6　　The LORD preserves ᵃthe simple;
　　I was ᵇbrought low, and He saved me.
7　　Return to your ᵃrest, O my soul,
　　For the LORD has ᵇdealt bountifully with you.
8　　For You have ᵃrescued my soul from death,
　　My eyes from tears,
　　My feet from stumbling.
9　　I shall walk before the LORD
　　In the ¹ᵃland of the living.
10　　I ᵃbelieved when I said,
　　"I am ᵇgreatly afflicted."
11　　I ᵃsaid in my alarm,

אֲהַבְתִּי כִּי־יִשְׁמַע ׀ יְהוָה **Psa. 116:1**
אֶת־קוֹלִי תַּחֲנוּנָי׃ ² כִּי־הִטָּה אָזְנוֹ
לִי וּבְיָמַי אֶקְרָא׃ ³ אֲפָפוּנִי ׀
חֶבְלֵי־מָוֶת וּמְצָרֵי שְׁאוֹל מְצָאוּנִי
צָרָה וְיָגוֹן אֶמְצָא׃ ⁴ וּבְשֵׁם־יְהוָה
אֶקְרָא אָנָּה יְהוָה מַלְּטָה נַפְשִׁי׃ ⁵
חַנּוּן יְהוָה וְצַדִּיק וֵאלֹהֵינוּ מְרַחֵם׃
⁶ שֹׁמֵר פְּתָאיִם יְהוָה דַּלּוֹתִי וְלִי
יְהוֹשִׁיעַ׃ ⁷ שׁוּבִי נַפְשִׁי לִמְנוּחָיְכִי
כִּי־יְהוָה גָּמַל עָלָיְכִי׃ ⁸ כִּי חִלַּצְתָּ
נַפְשִׁי מִמָּוֶת אֶת־עֵינִי מִן־דִּמְעָה
אֶת־רַגְלִי מִדֶּחִי׃ ⁹ אֶתְהַלֵּךְ לִפְנֵי
יְהוָה בְּאַרְצוֹת הַחַיִּים׃ ¹⁰ הֶאֱמַנְתִּי
כִּי אֲדַבֵּר אֲנִי עָנִיתִי מְאֹד׃ ¹¹ אֲנִי
אָמַרְתִּי בְחָפְזִי כָּל־הָאָדָם כֹּזֵב׃ ¹²
מָה־אָשִׁיב לַיהוָה כָּל־תַּגְמוּלוֹהִי
עָלָי׃ ¹³ כּוֹס־יְשׁוּעוֹת אֶשָּׂא וּבְשֵׁם
יְהוָה אֶקְרָא׃ ¹⁴ נְדָרַי לַיהוָה
אֲשַׁלֵּם נֶגְדָה־נָּא לְכָל־עַמּוֹ׃ ¹⁵ יָקָר
בְּעֵינֵי יְהוָה הַמָּוְתָה לַחֲסִידָיו׃ ¹⁶
אָנָּה יְהוָה כִּי־אֲנִי עַבְדֶּךָ אֲנִי־
עַבְדְּךָ בֶּן־אֲמָתֶךָ פִּתַּחְתָּ לְמוֹסֵרָי׃
¹⁷ לְךָ־אֶזְבַּח זֶבַח תּוֹדָה וּבְשֵׁם יְהוָה
אֶקְרָא׃ ¹⁸ נְדָרַי לַיהוָה אֲשַׁלֵּם

*"[b]*All men are liars."

Psa. 116:12   What shall I [a]render to the LORD
For all His [b]benefits [1]toward me?
13   I shall lift up the [a]cup of salvation
And [b]call upon the name of the LORD.
14   I shall [a]pay my vows to the LORD,
Oh *may it be* [b]in the presence of all His people.
15   [a]Precious in the sight of the LORD
Is the death of His godly ones.
16   O LORD, [1]surely I am [a]Your servant,
I am Your servant, the [b]son of Your handmaid,
You have [c]loosed my bonds.
17   To You I shall offer [a]a sacrifice of thanksgiving,
And [b]call upon the name of the LORD.
18   I shall [a]pay my vows to the LORD,
Oh *may it be* in the presence of all His people,
19   In the [a]courts of the LORD'S house,
In the midst of you, O [b]Jerusalem.
[1]Praise [2]the LORD!

נֶגְדָה־נָּא לְכָל־עַמּוֹ ׃ [19] בְּחַצְרוֹת ׀
בֵּית יְהוָה בְּתוֹכֵכִי יְרוּשָׁלָ͏ִם הַלְלוּ־
יָהּ ׃

References

Psalm 116:1
*a*Ps 18:1
*b*Ps 6:8; 66:19; Is 37:17; Dan 9:18

Psalm 116:2
*a*Ps 17:6; 31:2; 40:1

Psalm 116:3
[1]Lit *straits*
[2]I.e. the nether world
[3]Lit *found me*
*a*Ps 18:4, 5

Psalm 116:4
[1]Or *deliver my soul*
*a*Ps 18:6; 118:5
*b*Ps 17:13; 22:20

Psalm 116:5
*a*Ps 86:15; 103:8
*b*Ezra 9:15; Neh 9:8; Ps 119:137; 145:17; Jer 12:1; Dan 9:14
*c*Ex 34:6

Psalm 116:6
*a*Ps 19:7; Prov 1:4
*b*Ps 79:8; 142:6

Psalm 116:7
*a*Jer 6:16; Matt 11:29
*b*Ps 13:6; 142:7

Psalm 116:8
*a*Ps 49:15; 56:13; 86:13

Psalm 116:9
[1]Lit *lands*
*a*Ps 27:13

Psalm 116:10
[a]2 Cor 4:13
[b]Ps 88:7

Psalm 116:11
[a]Ps 31:22
[b]Ps 62:9; Rom 3:4

Psalm 116:12
[1]Lit *upon*
[a]2 Chr 32:25; 1 Thess 3:9
[b]Ps 103:2

Psalm 116:13
[a]Ps 16:5
[b]Ps 80:18; 105:1

Psalm 116:14
[a]Ps 50:14; 116:18
[b]Ps 22:25

Psalm 116:15
[a]Ps 72:14

Psalm 116:16
[1]Or *because*
[a]Ps 86:16; 119:125; 143:12
[b]Ps 86:16
[c]Ps 107:14

Psalm 116:17
[a]Lev 7:12; Ps 50:14
[b]Ps 116:13

Psalm 116:18
[a]Ps 116:14

Psalm 116:19
[1]Or *Hallelujah!*
[2]Heb *YAH*

[a] Ps 92:13; 96:8; 135:2
[b] Ps 102:21

Targum

Psa. 116:1 I love, for the LORD will hear my voice, my prayer. ² For he has inclined his ear to me, and I call [to him] throughout my days. ³ The sicknesses of death surrounded me, and the pains of Sheol found me; pain and sorrow I will find. ⁴ And in the name of the LORD I will call out: Please, O LORD, save my soul. ⁵ The LORD is gracious and righteous, and our God is merciful. ⁶ The LORD observes enticements; I became poor, and it was meet to redeem me. ⁷ Return, O my soul, to your place of rest, for the word of the LORD has repaid you with good. ⁸ For you have delivered my soul from being killed, my eyes from tears, my feet from stumbling. ⁹ I will walk before the LORD in the land of the living. ¹⁰ I have believed, therefore I will speak; in the assembly of the righteous I have sung much praise. ¹¹ I said when I fled, "All the sons of men are liars." ¹² How will I repay in the presence of the LORD all his kind favors that are shown to me? ¹³ The cup of redemption I will carry in the age to come, and I will call on the name of the LORD. ¹⁴ I will repay my vows in the presence of the LORD, I will tell now his miracles to all his people. ¹⁵ Honorable in the presence of the LORD is the death that is sent to his pious ones. ¹⁶ Please, O LORD; for I am your servant; I am your servant, the son of your handmaiden, you have loosened my bonds. ¹⁷ To you I will sacrifice the sacrifice of slaughter, and call out in the name of the LORD. ¹⁸ I will repay my vows in the presence of the LORD, I will tell now his miracles to all his people. ¹⁹ In the courts of the sanctuary of our God, in your midst, O Jerusalem. Hallelujah!

Spiritual Awareness

Introduction

This Psalm of David starts with David saying that he loved the LORD because he knew that the LORD was hearing his voice. Despite the harassment that Saul was doing, David placed his love in the LORD's protection. When a messenger brought David the news that Saul was dead, he was greatly disturbed. The man boasted that he killed David's enemy. David ordered the man to be executed because Saul was the anointed of the LORD (2 Samuel 1:14).

The Talmud in Rosh Hashanah (16b-17a) explains that this Psalm is about the Final Judgment at the end of time. There is to be a Great Resurrection of the dead at that time. The average people will be saved from Sheol because the LORD will hear their cries and will forgive them.

Notes on the Psalm

Verse eighteen is an important verse to remember. One must fulfill vows made to the LORD. Numerous times people make agreements with the LORD in that they will do something for the LORD if the LORD does something for them. Most of the time, the person making the vow does not fulfill their part of the agreement. It is imperative that if a person takes a vow that the person completes it before judgment day. Since no one knows how long they will live, it is imperative to fulfill all committed vows.

Psalm 117

New American Standard 1995	Hebrew
Psa. 117:1 ^aPraise the LORD, all nations; Laud Him, all peoples! 2 For His ^alovingkindness ¹is great toward us, And the ^{2b}truth of the LORD is everlasting. ³Praise ⁴the LORD!	הַלְלוּ אֶת־יְהוָה כָּל־גּוֹיִם **Psa. 117:1** שַׁבְּחוּהוּ כָּל־הָאֻמִּים ׃ 2 כִּי גָבַר עָלֵינוּ ׀ חַסְדּוֹ וֶאֱמֶת־יְהוָה לְעוֹלָם הַלְלוּ־יָהּ ׃

References

Psalm 117:1
[a]Rom 15:11

Psalm 117:2
[1]Lit *prevails over us*
[2]Or *faithfulness*
[3]Or *Hallelujah!*
[4]Heb *YAH*
[a]Ps 103:11
[b]Ps 100:5; 146:6

Targum

Psa. 117:1 Praise the LORD, all you Gentiles; praise him, all you nations. [2] For he has increased his goodness towards us; and the truth of the LORD is forever. Hallelujah!

Spiritual Awareness

Introduction

The Sage Radak said that the brevity of the Psalm symbolizes the simplicity of the world order when the Messiah comes. In the future, there will be two groups of people: the Children of Israel who follow Torah and the rest who follow the Torah's seven Noachide laws.

"The 7 Noahide Laws are rules that all of us must keep, regardless of who we are or from where we come. Without these seven things, it would be impossible for humanity to live together in harmony.

1. **Do not profane G-d's Oneness in any way.** Acknowledge that there is a single <u>G-d</u> who cares about what we are doing and desires that we take care of His world.

2. **Do not curse your Creator.** No matter how angry you may be, do not take it out verbally against your Creator.

3. **Do not murder.** The value of human life cannot be measured. To destroy a single human life is to destroy the entire world—because, for that person, the world has ceased to exist. It follows that by sustaining a single human life, you are sustaining an entire universe.

4. **Do not eat a limb of a still-living animal.** Respect the life of all G-d's creatures. As intelligent beings, we have a duty not to cause undue pain to other creatures.

5. **Do not steal.** Whatever benefits you receive in this world, make sure that none of them are at the unfair expense of someone else.

6. **Harness and channel the human libido.** Incest, adultery, rape and homosexual relations are forbidden. The family unit is the foundation of human society. Sexuality is the fountain of life and so nothing is more holy than the sexual act. So, too, when abused, nothing can be more debasing and destructive to the human being.

7. **Establish courts of law and ensure justice in our world.** With every small act of justice, we are restoring harmony to our world, synchronizing it with a supernal order. That is why we must keep the laws established by our government for the country's stability and harmony.

These laws were communicated by G-d to Adam and Noah, ancestors of all human beings. That is what makes these rules universal, for all times, places and people:

Laws made by humans may change according to circumstance. But laws made by the Creator of all souls over all of time remain the same for all people at all times..

If we would fulfill these laws just because they make sense to us, then we would change them, according to our convenience. We would be our own god. But when we understand that they are the laws of a supreme G-d, we understand that they can not be changed, just as He does not change."[1]

---

[1] "The 7 Noahide Laws: Universal Morality - Chabad.org," accessed February 17, 2023, https://www.chabad.org/library/article_cdo/aid/62221/jewish/The-7-Noahide-Laws-Universal-Morality.htm.

Psalm 118

New American Standard 1995	Hebrew
Psa. 118:1 *ᵃ*Give thanks to the LORD, for *ᵇ*He is good; For His lovingkindness is everlasting. 2 Oh let *ᶜ*Israel say, "His lovingkindness is everlasting." 3 Oh let the *ᵈ*house of Aaron say, "His lovingkindness is everlasting." 4 Oh let those *ᵃ*who ¹fear the LORD say, "His lovingkindness is everlasting." **Psa. 118:5** From *my* *ᵃ*distress I called upon ¹the LORD; ¹The LORD answered me *and* *ᵇ*set *me* in a large place. 6 The LORD is *ᵃ*for me; I will *ᵇ*not fear; *ᶜ*What can man do to me? 7 The LORD is for me *ᵃ*among those who help me; Therefore I will *ᵇ*look *with satisfaction* on those who hate me. 8 It is *ᵃ*better to take refuge in the LORD Than to trust in man. 9 It is *ᵃ*better to take refuge in the LORD Than to trust in princes. **Psa. 118:10** All nations *ᵃ*surrounded me;	**Psa. 118:1** הוֹדוּ לַיהֹוָה כִּי־טוֹב כִּי לְעוֹלָם חַסְדּוֹ ׃ 2 יֹאמַר־נָא 3 ׃ יִשְׂרָאֵל כִּי לְעוֹלָם חַסְדּוֹ יֹאמְרוּ־נָא בֵית־אַהֲרֹן כִּי לְעוֹלָם חַסְדּוֹ ׃ 4 יֹאמְרוּ־נָא 5 ׃ יִרְאֵי יְהֹוָה כִּי לְעוֹלָם חַסְדּוֹ מִן־הַמֵּצַר קָרָאתִי יָּהּ עָנָנִי בַמֶּרְחָב יָהּ ׃ 6 יְהֹוָה לִי לֹא 7 ׃ אִירָא מַה־יַּעֲשֶׂה לִי אָדָם יְהֹוָה לִי בְּעֹזְרָי וַאֲנִי אֶרְאֶה בְשֹׂנְאָי ׃ 8 טוֹב לַחֲסוֹת בַּיהֹוָה מִבְּטֹחַ בָּאָדָם ׃ 9 טוֹב לַחֲסוֹת בַּיהֹוָה מִבְּטֹחַ בִּנְדִיבִים ׃ 10 כָּל־ גּוֹיִם סְבָבוּנִי בְּשֵׁם יְהֹוָה כִּי אֲמִילַם ׃ 11 סַבּוּנִי גַם־סְבָבוּנִי בְּשֵׁם יְהֹוָה כִּי אֲמִילַם ׃ 12 סַבּוּנִי כִדְבוֹרִים דֹּעֲכוּ כְּאֵשׁ קוֹצִים בְּשֵׁם יְהֹוָה כִּי אֲמִילַם ׃ 13 דַּחֹה דְחִיתַנִי לִנְפֹּל וַיהֹוָה עֲזָרָנִי ׃ 14 עָזִּי וְזִמְרָת יָהּ וַיְהִי־לִי לִישׁוּעָה ׃ 15 קוֹל רִנָּה וִישׁוּעָה

In the name of the LORD I will surely [b]cut them off.

11 They [a]surrounded me, yes, they surrounded me;

In the name of the LORD I will surely cut them off.

12 They surrounded me [a]like bees;

They were extinguished as a [b]fire of thorns;

In the name of the LORD I will surely cut them off.

13 You [a]pushed me violently so that I [1]was falling,

But the LORD [b]helped me.

14 [1a]The LORD is my strength and song,

And He has become [b]my salvation.

Psa. 118:15 The sound of [a]joyful shouting and salvation is in the tents of the righteous;

The [b]right hand of the LORD does valiantly.

16 The [a]right hand of the LORD is exalted;

The right hand of the LORD does valiantly.

17 I [a]will not die, but live,

And [b]tell of the works of [1]the LORD.

18 [1]The LORD has [a]disciplined me severely,

But He has [b]not given me over to death.

Psa. 118:19 [a]Open to me the gates of righteousness;

I shall enter through them, I shall give thanks to [1]the LORD.

20 This is the gate of the LORD;

בְּאָהֳלֵי צַדִּיקִים יְמִין יְהוָה
16 : יְמִין יְהוָה רוֹמֵמָה
17 : יְמִין יְהוָה עֹשָׂה חָיִל : לֹא
אָמוּת כִּי־אֶחְיֶה וַאֲסַפֵּר מַעֲשֵׂי
18 : יָהּ יַסֹּר יִסְּרַנִּי יָּהּ וְלַמָּוֶת לֹא
19 : נְתָנָנִי פִּתְחוּ־לִי שַׁעֲרֵי־צֶדֶק
20 : אָבֹא־בָם אוֹדֶה יָהּ זֶה־
הַשַּׁעַר לַיהוָה צַדִּיקִים יָבֹאוּ
21 : בוֹ אוֹדְךָ כִּי עֲנִיתָנִי וַתְּהִי־
22 : לִי לִישׁוּעָה אֶבֶן מָאֲסוּ
23 : הַבּוֹנִים הָיְתָה לְרֹאשׁ פִּנָּה
מֵאֵת יְהוָה הָיְתָה זֹּאת הִיא
24 : נִפְלָאת בְּעֵינֵינוּ זֶה־הַיּוֹם
עָשָׂה יְהוָה נָגִילָה וְנִשְׂמְחָה בוֹ :
25 אָנָּא יְהוָה הוֹשִׁיעָה נָּא אָנָּא
26 : יְהוָה הַצְלִיחָה נָּא בָּרוּךְ
הַבָּא בְּשֵׁם יְהוָה בֵּרַכְנוּכֶם
27 : מִבֵּית יְהוָה אֵל יְהוָה וַיָּאֶר
לָנוּ אִסְרוּ־חַג בַּעֲבֹתִים עַד־
28 : קַרְנוֹת הַמִּזְבֵּחַ אֵלִי אַתָּה
29 : וְאוֹדֶךָּ אֱלֹהַי אֲרוֹמְמֶךָּ הוֹדוּ
לַיהוָה כִּי־טוֹב כִּי לְעוֹלָם חַסְדּוֹ :

The *a*righteous will enter through it.

21   I shall give thanks to You, for You have *a*answered me,

And You have *b*become my salvation.

Psa. 118:22   The *a*stone which the builders rejected

Has become the chief corner *stone*.

23   This is [1]the LORD'S doing;

It is marvelous in our eyes.

24   This is the day which the LORD has made;

Let us *a*rejoice and be glad in it.

25   O LORD, *a*do save, we beseech You;

O LORD, we beseech You, do send *b*prosperity!

26   *a*Blessed is the one who comes in the name of the LORD;

We have *b*blessed you from the house of the LORD.

27   *a*The LORD is God, and He has given us *b*light;

Bind the festival sacrifice with cords [1]to the *c*horns of the altar.

28   *a*You are my God, and I give thanks to You;

You are my God, *b*I extol You.

29   *a*Give thanks to the LORD, for He is good;

For His lovingkindness is everlasting.

References

Psalm 118:1
[a]1 Chr 16:8, 34; Ps 106:1; 107:1; Jer 33:11
[b]2 Chr 5:13; 7:3; Ezra 3:11; Ps 100:5; 136:1-26

Psalm 118:2
[a]Ps 115:9

Psalm 118:3
[a]Ps 115:10

Psalm 118:4
[1]Or *revere*
[a]Ps 115:11

Psalm 118:5
[1]Heb *YAH*
[a]Ps 18:6; 86:7; 120:1
[b]Ps 18:19

Psalm 118:6
[a]Job 19:27; Ps 56:9; Heb 13:6
[b]Ps 23:4; 27:1
[c]Ps 56:4, 11

Psalm 118:7
[a]Ps 54:4
[b]Ps 54:7; 59:10

Psalm 118:8
[a]2 Chr 32:7, 8; Ps 40:4; 108:12; Is 31:1, 3; 57:13; Jer 17:5

Psalm 118:9
[a]Ps 146:3

Psalm 118:10
[a]Ps 3:6; 88:17
[b]Ps 18:40

Psalm 118:11

*a*Ps 88:17

Psalm 118:12
*a*Deut 1:44
*b*Ps 58:9; Nah 1:10

Psalm 118:13
[1]Or *fell*
*a*Ps 140:4
*b*Ps 86:17

Psalm 118:14
[1]Heb *YAH*
*a*Ex 15:2; Is 12:2
*b*Ps 27:1

Psalm 118:15
*a*Ps 68:3
*b*Ex 15:6; Ps 89:13; Luke 1:51

Psalm 118:16
*a*Ex 15:6; Ps 89:13

Psalm 118:17
[1]Heb *YAH*
*a*Ps 6:5; 116:8, 9; Hab 1:12
*b*Ps 73:28; 107:22

Psalm 118:18
[1]Heb *YAH*
*a*Ps 73:14; Jer 31:18; 1 Cor 11:32; 2 Cor 6:9
*b*Ps 86:13

Psalm 118:19
[1]Heb *YAH*
*a*Is 26:2

Psalm 118:20
*a*Ps 15:1, 2; 24:3-6; 140:13; Is 35:8; Rev 22:14

Psalm 118:21

[a]Ps 116:1; 118:5
[b]Ps 118:14

Psalm 118:22
[a]Matt 21:42; Mark 12:10, 11; Luke 20:17; Acts 4:11; Eph 2:20; 1 Pet 2:7

Psalm 118:23
[1]Lit *from the LORD*

Psalm 118:24
[a]Ps 31:7

Psalm 118:25
[a]Ps 106:47
[b]Ps 122:6, 7

Psalm 118:26
[a]Matt 21:9; 23:39; Mark 11:9; Luke 13:35; 19:38; John 12:13
[b]Ps 129:8

Psalm 118:27
[1]Lit *unto*
[a]1 Kin 18:39
[b]Esth 8:16; Ps 18:28; 27:1; 1 Pet 2:9
[c]Ex 27:2

Psalm 118:28
[a]Ps 63:1; 140:6
[b]Ex 15:2; Is 25:1

Psalm 118:29
[a]Ps 118:1

Targum

Psa. 118:1 Sing praise in the presence of the LORD, for he is good, for his goodness is forever. [2] Let Israel now say, "For his goodness is forever." [3] Let the house of Aaron now say, "For his goodness is forever." [4] Let those who fear the LORD now say, "For his goodness is forever." [5] Out of distress I called to Yah, Yah accepted my prayer in a broad place. [6] The word of the LORD is my help, I will not fear, what will a son of man do to me? [7] The word of the LORD is helping me, and I will behold, vengeance on my foes. [8] It is better to trust in the word of the LORD than to rely on a son of man. [9] It is better to trust in the word of the LORD than to rely on rulers. [10] All the Gentiles have surrounded me; in the name of the word of the LORD I have put my trust, for I will tear them apart. [11] They have encompassed me, indeed, surrounded me; in the name of the word of the LORD I have put my trust, for I will tear them apart. [12] They have encompassed me like hornets; they burned like fire in thorns; in the name of the word of the LORD I have put my trust, for I will tear them apart. [13] But you have knocked me down to make me fall; and the word of the LORD has given me help. [14] My strength and my praise are fearful against all the world; the LORD gave command by his word, and has become my redeemer. [15] The sound of praise and redemption is in the tents of the righteous; the right hand of the LORD has done mightily. [16] The right hand of the LORD is exalted; the right hand of the LORD has done mightily. [17] I will not die, for I will live, and I will tell of the deeds of God. [18] Truly, has Yah punished me, but he did not hand me over to death. [19] Open to me the entrances of the city of righteousness; I will enter them, I will praise Yah. [20] This is the entrance of the sanctuary of the LORD; the righteous will enter by it. [21] I will give thanks in your presence, for you have received my prayer, and become for me a redeemer. [22] The child the builders abandoned was among the sons of Jesse; and he was worthy to be appointed king and ruler. [23] "This has come from the presence of the LORD," said the builders; "it is wonderful before us," said the sons of Jesse. [24] "This day the LORD has made," said the builders; "let us rejoice and be glad in it," said the sons of Jesse. [25] "If it please you, O LORD, redeem us now," said the builders; "if it please you, O LORD, prosper us now," said Jesse and his wife. [26] "Blessed is he who comes in the name of the word of the LORD," said the builders; "they will bless you from the sanctuary of the LORD," said David. [27] "God, the LORD, has given us light," said the tribes of the house of Judah; "bind the child for a festal sacrifice with chains until you sacrifice him, and sprinkle his blood on the horns of the altar," said Samuel the prophet. [28] "You are my God, and I will give thanks in your presence; my God, I will praise you," said David. [29] Samuel answered and said, "Sing praise, assembly of Israel, give thanks in the presence of the LORD, for he is good, for his goodness is everlasting."

Spiritual Awareness

Introduction

The Sage Radak saw two levels of interpretation for this Psalm. At the personal level, David expresses his relief that Saul's persecution of him ends with Saul's death. David also envisioned the improvements he wanted to make for the nation. At a national level, this Psalm reflects the joy by which Israel will experience at the final redemption. Israel will return to its former glory and some of the old traditions and institutions will be restored.

Verse one through four

The Psalmist acknowledges that the lovingkindness of the LORD from the Sefirah Chesed will last throughout all time.

Acknowledge it to the LORD that the Sefirah Chesed will send his lovingkindness forever.

Say it now O Israel, that the Sefirah Chesed endures forever.

Say it now, O House of Aharon that the Sefirah Chesed endures forever.

Say it now, I those who fear the LORD that the Sefirah Chesed endures forever.

Verse nineteen and twenty

The Psalmist is referring to the fifty gates.

"Fifty Gates of Understanding were created in the world, and 49 were give to Moshe Rabbeinu. (Rosh Hashanah 21b)

The "Fifty Gates of Understanding" represent 50 spiritual channels, if you will, through which the Divine light of understanding makes its way from the upper realm to the lower realms. The gates themselves are the basis of all of Torah, and just achieving a few of the "gates" would make one a wise person. Receiving 49 of the 50 gates is beyond our present level of comprehension, but suffice it to say that it would, and did, make Moshe Rabbeinu other-worldly: Rebi Noson says: The intention of the Torah was that [Moshe] might be purged of all food and drink in his bowels so as to make him equal to the ministering angels. (Yoma 4b)

The so-called burial place of Moshe Rabbeinu itself bears witness to an even greater accomplishment. The Torah tells us where Moshe Rabbeinu was buried:
And Moshe went up from the plains of Moav to Mount Nevo, [to the] top of the summit facing Jericho.(Devarim 34:1)

Was "Nevo" merely the name of the mountain? Apparently it tells us more than the physical location of Moshe Rabbeinu's burial:
Before his death he merited the 50th gate [of understanding], as it says, "To Mt. Nevo" (Devarim34:1): Nun Bo; the Nun entered his name and it became Neshamah. (Kehillas Ya'akov)

In other words, the letter Nun, which represents the number 50 and the level of Divine light associated with it, became a part of Moshe's name, which is spelled

Moshe-Shin-Heh. With the addition of the letter Nun from the Nun Sha'arei Binah—the Fifty Gates of Understanding—the word can spell "Neshamah," the third highest level of soul that we can access at this time."[2]

Open for me the gates of righteousness; I will enter into them and acknowledge God.

This gate is the LORD's, the righteous shall enter into it.

[2] Rabbi Pinchas Winston, "Fifty Gates of Understanding," Torah.org, October 1, 2014, https://torah.org/torah-portion/perceptions-5775-zoshabracha/.

Psalm 119

New American Standard 1995	Hebrew

Psa. 119:1 How blessed are those whose way is [1][a]blameless,

Who [b]walk in the law of the LORD.

2 How blessed are those who [a]observe His testimonies,

Who [b]seek Him [c]with all *their* heart.

3 They also [a]do no unrighteousness;
They walk in His ways.

4 You have [1][a]ordained Your precepts,

[2]That we should keep *them* diligently.

5 Oh that my [a]ways may be established
To [b]keep Your statutes!

6 Then I [a]shall not be ashamed
When I look [1]upon all Your commandments.

7 I shall [a]give thanks to You with uprightness of heart,

When I learn Your righteous judgments.

8 I shall keep Your statutes;
Do not [a]forsake me utterly!

Psa. 119:9 How can a young man keep his way pure?

By [a]keeping *it* according to Your word.

10 With [a]all my heart I have sought You;

Do not let me [b]wander from Your commandments.

11 Your word I have [a]treasured in my heart,

אַשְׁרֵי תְמִימֵי־דָרֶךְ הַהֹלְכִים **Psa. 119:1**

בְּתוֹרַת יְהוָה׃ 2 אַשְׁרֵי נֹצְרֵי עֵדֹתָיו

בְּכָל־לֵב יִדְרְשׁוּהוּ׃ 3 אַף לֹא־פָעֲלוּ

עַוְלָה בִּדְרָכָיו הָלָכוּ׃ 4 אַתָּה צִוִּיתָה

פִקֻּדֶיךָ לִשְׁמֹר מְאֹד׃ 5 אַחֲלַי יִכֹּנוּ

דְרָכָי לִשְׁמֹר חֻקֶּיךָ׃ 6 אָז לֹא־אֵבוֹשׁ

בְּהַבִּיטִי אֶל־כָּל־מִצְוֺתֶיךָ׃ 7 אוֹדְךָ

בְּיֹשֶׁר לֵבָב בְּלָמְדִי מִשְׁפְּטֵי צִדְקֶךָ׃ 8

אֶת־חֻקֶּיךָ אֶשְׁמֹר אַל־תַּעַזְבֵנִי עַד־

מְאֹד׃ 9 בַּמֶּה יְזַכֶּה־נַּעַר אֶת־אָרְחוֹ

לִשְׁמֹר כִּדְבָרֶךָ׃ 10 בְּכָל־לִבִּי דְרַשְׁתִּיךָ

אַל־תַּשְׁגֵּנִי מִמִּצְוֺתֶיךָ׃ 11 בְּלִבִּי צָפַנְתִּי

אִמְרָתֶךָ לְמַעַן לֹא אֶחֱטָא־לָךְ׃ 12

בָּרוּךְ אַתָּה יְהוָה לַמְּדֵנִי חֻקֶּיךָ׃ 13

בִּשְׂפָתַי סִפַּרְתִּי כֹּל מִשְׁפְּטֵי־פִיךָ׃ 14

בְּדֶרֶךְ עֵדְוֺתֶיךָ שַׂשְׂתִּי כְּעַל כָּל־הוֹן׃ 15

בְּפִקֻּדֶיךָ אָשִׂיחָה וְאַבִּיטָה אֹרְחֹתֶיךָ׃ 16

בְּחֻקֹּתֶיךָ אֶשְׁתַּעֲשָׁע לֹא אֶשְׁכַּח דְּבָרֶךָ׃

17 גְּמֹל עַל־עַבְדְּךָ אֶחְיֶה וְאֶשְׁמְרָה

דְבָרֶךָ׃ 18 גַּל־עֵינַי וְאַבִּיטָה נִפְלָאוֹת

מִתּוֹרָתֶךָ׃ 19 גֵּר אָנֹכִי בָאָרֶץ אַל־

תַּסְתֵּר מִמֶּנִּי מִצְוֺתֶיךָ׃ 20 גָּרְסָה נַפְשִׁי

לְתַאֲבָה אֶל־מִשְׁפָּטֶיךָ בְכָל־עֵת׃ 21

גָּעַרְתָּ זֵדִים אֲרוּרִים הַשֹּׁגִים מִמִּצְוֺתֶיךָ׃

22 גַּל מֵעָלַי חֶרְפָּה וָבוּז כִּי עֵדֹתֶיךָ

נָצָרְתִּי׃ 23 גַּם יָשְׁבוּ שָׂרִים בִּי נִדְבָּרוּ

עַבְדְּךָ יָשִׂיחַ בְּחֻקֶּיךָ׃ 24 גַּם־עֵדֹתֶיךָ

שַׁעֲשֻׁעָי אַנְשֵׁי עֲצָתִי׃ 25 דָּבְקָה לֶעָפָר

<table>
<tr><td valign="top">

12

13

14

15

16

</td><td valign="top">

That I may not sin against You.
Blessed are You, O LORD;
[a]Teach me Your statutes.
With my lips I have [a]told of
All the [b]ordinances of Your mouth.
I have [a]rejoiced in the way of Your testimonies,
[1]As much as in all riches.
I will [a]meditate on Your precepts
And [1]regard [b]Your ways.
I shall [1a]delight in Your statutes;
I shall [b]not forget Your word.

</td><td valign="top">

נַפְשִׁי חַוֵּנִי כִדְבָרֶךָ ׃ 26 דְּרָכַי סִפַּרְתִּי
וַתַּעֲנֵנִי לַמְּדֵנִי חֻקֶּיךָ ׃ 27 דֶּרֶךְ־פִּקּוּדֶיךָ
הֲבִינֵנִי וְאָשִׂיחָה בְּנִפְלְאוֹתֶיךָ ׃ 28
דָּלְפָה נַפְשִׁי מִתּוּגָה קַיְּמֵנִי כִּדְבָרֶךָ ׃ 29
דֶּרֶךְ־שֶׁקֶר הָסֵר מִמֶּנִּי וְתוֹרָתְךָ חָנֵּנִי ׃
30 דֶּרֶךְ־אֱמוּנָה בָחָרְתִּי מִשְׁפָּטֶיךָ
שִׁוִּיתִי ׃ 31 דָּבַקְתִּי בְעֵדְוֺתֶיךָ יְהוָה אַל־
תְּבִישֵׁנִי ׃ 32 דֶּרֶךְ־מִצְוֺתֶיךָ אָרוּץ כִּי
תַרְחִיב לִבִּי ׃ 33 הוֹרֵנִי יְהוָה דֶּרֶךְ
חֻקֶּיךָ וְאֶצְּרֶנָּה עֵקֶב ׃ 34 הֲבִינֵנִי וְאֶצְּרָה
תוֹרָתֶךָ וְאֶשְׁמְרֶנָּה בְכָל־לֵב ׃ 35
הַדְרִיכֵנִי בִּנְתִיב מִצְוֺתֶיךָ כִּי־בוֹ
חָפָצְתִּי ׃ 36 הַט־לִבִּי אֶל־עֵדְוֺתֶיךָ וְאַל
אֶל־בָּצַע ׃ 37 הַעֲבֵר עֵינַי מֵרְאוֹת שָׁוְא
בִּדְרָכֶךָ חַיֵּנִי ׃ 38 הָקֵם לְעַבְדְּךָ
אִמְרָתֶךָ אֲשֶׁר לְיִרְאָתֶךָ ׃ 39 הַעֲבֵר
חֶרְפָּתִי אֲשֶׁר יָגֹרְתִּי כִּי מִשְׁפָּטֶיךָ
טוֹבִים ׃ 40 הִנֵּה תָּאַבְתִּי לְפִקֻּדֶיךָ

</td></tr>
<tr><td valign="top">

</td><td valign="top">

Psa. 119:17 [a]Deal bountifully with Your servant,
That I may live and keep Your word.

18 Open my eyes, that I may behold
Wonderful things from Your law.

19 I am a [a]stranger in the earth;
Do not hide Your commandments from me.

20 My soul is crushed [1a]with longing
After Your ordinances at all times.

21 You [a]rebuke the arrogant, [1]the [b]cursed,
Who [c]wander from Your commandments.

22 [a]Take away reproach and contempt from me,
For I [b]observe Your testimonies.

23 Even though [a]princes sit *and* talk against me,
Your servant [b]meditates on Your statutes.

24 Your testimonies also are my [a]delight;
They are [1]my counselors.

Psa. 119:25 My [a]soul cleaves to the dust;

</td><td valign="top">

בְּצִדְקָתֶךָ חַיֵּנִי ׃ 41 וִיבֹאֻנִי חֲסָדֶךָ יְהוָה
תְּשׁוּעָתְךָ כְּאִמְרָתֶךָ ׃ 42 וְאֶעֱנֶה חֹרְפִי
דָבָר כִּי־בָטַחְתִּי בִּדְבָרֶךָ ׃ 43 וְאַל־תַּצֵּל
מִפִּי דְבַר־אֱמֶת עַד־מְאֹד כִּי לְמִשְׁפָּטֶךָ
יִחָלְתִּי ׃ 44 וְאֶשְׁמְרָה תוֹרָתְךָ תָמִיד
לְעוֹלָם וָעֶד ׃ 45 וְאֶתְהַלְּכָה בָרְחָבָה כִּי
פִקֻּדֶיךָ דָרָשְׁתִּי ׃ 46 וַאֲדַבְּרָה בְעֵדֹתֶיךָ
נֶגֶד מְלָכִים וְלֹא אֵבוֹשׁ ׃ 47 וְאֶשְׁתַּעֲשַׁע
בְּמִצְוֺתֶיךָ אֲשֶׁר אָהָבְתִּי ׃ 48 וְאֶשָּׂא־כַפַּי
אֶל־מִצְוֺתֶיךָ אֲשֶׁר אָהָבְתִּי וְאָשִׂיחָה
בְחֻקֶּיךָ ׃ 49 זְכֹר־דָּבָר לְעַבְדֶּךָ עַל
אֲשֶׁר יִחַלְתָּנִי ׃ 50 זֹאת נֶחָמָתִי בְעָנְיִי כִּי
אִמְרָתְךָ חִיָּתְנִי ׃ 51 זֵדִים הֱלִיצֻנִי עַד־

</td></tr>
</table>

[b]Revive me [c]according to Your word.

26 I have told of my ways, and You have answered me;
[a]Teach me Your statutes.

27 Make me understand the way of Your precepts,
So I will [a]meditate on Your wonders.

28 My [a]soul [1]weeps because of grief;
[b]Strengthen me according to Your word.

29 Remove the false way from me,
And graciously grant me Your law.

30 I have chosen the faithful way;
I have [1]placed Your ordinances *before me.*

31 I [a]cling to Your testimonies;
O LORD, do not put me to shame!

32 I shall run the way of Your commandments,
For You will [a]enlarge my heart.

Psa. 119:33 [a]Teach me, O LORD, the way of Your statutes,
And I shall observe it to the end.

34 [a]Give me understanding, that I may [b]observe Your law
And keep it [c]with all *my* heart.

35 Make me walk in the [a]path of Your commandments,
For I [b]delight in it.

36 [a]Incline my heart to Your testimonies
And not to [b]*dishonest* gain.

37 Turn away my [a]eyes from looking at vanity,
And [b]revive me in Your ways.

38 [a]Establish Your [1]word to Your servant,

מֵאֹד מִתּוֹרָתְךָ לֹא נָטִיתִי׃ 52 זָכַרְתִּי
מִשְׁפָּטֶיךָ מֵעוֹלָם ׀ יְהוָה וָאֶתְנֶחָם׃ 53
זַלְעָפָה אֲחָזַתְנִי מֵרְשָׁעִים עֹזְבֵי
תּוֹרָתֶךָ׃ 54 זְמִרוֹת הָיוּ־לִי חֻקֶּיךָ בְּבֵית
מְגוּרָי׃ 55 זָכַרְתִּי בַלַּיְלָה שִׁמְךָ יְהוָה
וָאֶשְׁמְרָה תּוֹרָתֶךָ׃ 56 זֹאת הָיְתָה־לִּי כִּי
פִקֻּדֶיךָ נָצָרְתִּי׃ 57 חֶלְקִי יְהוָה אָמַרְתִּי
לִשְׁמֹר דְּבָרֶיךָ׃ 58 חִלִּיתִי פָנֶיךָ בְכָל־
לֵב חָנֵּנִי כְּאִמְרָתֶךָ׃ 59 חִשַּׁבְתִּי דְרָכָי
וָאָשִׁיבָה רַגְלַי אֶל־עֵדֹתֶיךָ׃ 60 חַשְׁתִּי
וְלֹא הִתְמַהְמָהְתִּי לִשְׁמֹר מִצְוֺתֶיךָ׃ 61
חֶבְלֵי רְשָׁעִים עִוְּדֻנִי תּוֹרָתְךָ לֹא
שָׁכָחְתִּי׃ 62 חֲצוֹת־לַיְלָה אָקוּם לְהוֹדוֹת
לָךְ עַל מִשְׁפְּטֵי צִדְקֶךָ׃ 63 חָבֵר אָנִי
לְכָל־אֲשֶׁר יְרֵאוּךָ וּלְשֹׁמְרֵי פִּקּוּדֶיךָ׃ 64
חַסְדְּךָ יְהוָה מָלְאָה הָאָרֶץ חֻקֶּיךָ
לַמְּדֵנִי׃ 65 טוֹב עָשִׂיתָ עִם־עַבְדְּךָ יְהוָה
כִּדְבָרֶךָ׃ 66 טוּב טַעַם וָדַעַת לַמְּדֵנִי כִּי
בְמִצְוֺתֶיךָ הֶאֱמָנְתִּי׃ 67 טֶרֶם אֶעֱנֶה אֲנִי
שֹׁגֵג וְעַתָּה אִמְרָתְךָ שָׁמָרְתִּי׃ 68 טוֹב־
אַתָּה וּמֵטִיב לַמְּדֵנִי חֻקֶּיךָ׃ 69 טָפְלוּ
עָלַי שֶׁקֶר זֵדִים אֲנִי בְּכָל־לֵב ׀ אֶצֹּר
פִּקּוּדֶיךָ׃ 70 טָפַשׁ כַּחֵלֶב לִבָּם אֲנִי
תּוֹרָתְךָ שִׁעֲשָׁעְתִּי׃ 71 טוֹב־לִי כִי־עֻנֵּיתִי
לְמַעַן אֶלְמַד חֻקֶּיךָ׃ 72 טוֹב־לִי תוֹרַת־
פִּיךָ מֵאַלְפֵי זָהָב וָכָסֶף׃ 73 יָדֶיךָ עָשׂוּנִי
וַיְכוֹנְנוּנִי הֲבִינֵנִי וְאֶלְמְדָה מִצְוֺתֶיךָ׃ 74
יְרֵאֶיךָ יִרְאוּנִי וְיִשְׂמָחוּ כִּי לִדְבָרְךָ
יִחָלְתִּי׃ 75 יָדַעְתִּי יְהוָה כִּי־צֶדֶק
מִשְׁפָּטֶיךָ וֶאֱמוּנָה עִנִּיתָנִי׃ 76 יְהִי־נָא
חַסְדְּךָ לְנַחֲמֵנִי כְּאִמְרָתְךָ לְעַבְדֶּךָ׃ 77

[2]As that which produces reverence for You.

39 [a]Turn away my reproach which I dread,

For Your ordinances are good.

40 Behold, I [a]long for Your precepts;
Revive me through Your righteousness.

Psa. 119:41 May Your [a]lovingkindnesses also come to me, O LORD,

Your salvation [b]according to Your [1]word;

42 So I will have an [a]answer for him who [b]reproaches me,

For I trust in Your word.

43 And do not take the word of truth utterly out of my mouth,

For I [1a]wait for Your ordinances.

44 So I will [a]keep Your law continually,

Forever and ever.

45 And I will [a]walk [1]at liberty,

For I [b]seek Your precepts.

46 I will also speak of Your testimonies [a]before kings

And shall not be ashamed.

47 I shall [1a]delight in Your commandments,

Which I [b]love.

48 And I shall lift up my hands to Your commandments,

Which I [a]love;

And I will [b]meditate on Your statutes.

Psa. 119:49 Remember the word to Your servant,

[1]In which You have made me hope.

יְבֹאוּנִי רַחֲמֶיךָ וְאֶחְיֶה כִּי־תוֹרָתְךָ

שַׁעֲשֻׁעָי ׃ 78 יֵבֹשׁוּ זֵדִים כִּי־שֶׁקֶר עִוְּתוּנִי

אֲנִי אָשִׂיחַ בְּפִקּוּדֶיךָ ׃ 79 יָשׁוּבוּ לִי

יְרֵאֶיךָ וְיֹדְעוּ [וְ][יֹדְעֵי] עֵדֹתֶיךָ ׃ 80

יְהִי־לִבִּי תָמִים בְּחֻקֶּיךָ לְמַעַן לֹא

אֵבוֹשׁ ׃ 81 כָּלְתָה לִתְשׁוּעָתְךָ נַפְשִׁי

לִדְבָרְךָ יִחָלְתִּי ׃ 82 כָּלוּ עֵינַי לְאִמְרָתֶךָ

לֵאמֹר מָתַי תְּנַחֲמֵנִי ׃ 83 כִּי־הָיִיתִי

כְּנֹאד בְּקִיטוֹר חֻקֶּיךָ לֹא שָׁכָחְתִּי ׃ 84

כַּמָּה יְמֵי־עַבְדֶּךָ מָתַי תַּעֲשֶׂה בְרֹדְפַי

מִשְׁפָּט ׃ 85 כָּרוּ־לִי זֵדִים שִׁיחוֹת אֲשֶׁר

לֹא כְתוֹרָתֶךָ ׃ 86 כָּל־מִצְוֹתֶיךָ אֱמוּנָה

שֶׁקֶר רְדָפוּנִי עָזְרֵנִי ׃ 87 כִּמְעַט כִּלּוּנִי

בָאָרֶץ וַאֲנִי לֹא־עָזַבְתִּי פִקּוּדֶיךָ ׃ 88

כְּחַסְדְּךָ חַיֵּנִי וְאֶשְׁמְרָה עֵדוּת פִּיךָ ׃ 89

לְעוֹלָם יְהוָה דְּבָרְךָ נִצָּב בַּשָּׁמָיִם ׃ 90

לְדֹר וָדֹר אֱמוּנָתֶךָ כּוֹנַנְתָּ אֶרֶץ

וַתַּעֲמֹד ׃ 91 לְמִשְׁפָּטֶיךָ עָמְדוּ הַיּוֹם כִּי

הַכֹּל עֲבָדֶיךָ ׃ 92 לוּלֵי תוֹרָתְךָ שַׁעֲשֻׁעָי

אָז אָבַדְתִּי בְעָנְיִי ׃ 93 לְעוֹלָם לֹא־

אֶשְׁכַּח פִּקּוּדֶיךָ כִּי בָם חִיִּיתָנִי ׃ 94 לְךָ־

אֲנִי הוֹשִׁיעֵנִי כִּי פִקּוּדֶיךָ דָרָשְׁתִּי ׃ 95

לִי קִוּוּ רְשָׁעִים לְאַבְּדֵנִי עֵדֹתֶיךָ

אֶתְבּוֹנָן ׃ 96 לְכָל־תִּכְלָה רָאִיתִי קֵץ

רְחָבָה מִצְוָתְךָ מְאֹד ׃ 97 מָה־אָהַבְתִּי

תוֹרָתֶךָ כָּל־הַיּוֹם הִיא שִׂיחָתִי ׃ 98

מֵאֹיְבַי תְּחַכְּמֵנִי מִצְוֹתֶךָ כִּי לְעוֹלָם

הִיא־לִי ׃ 99 מִכָּל־מְלַמְּדַי הִשְׂכַּלְתִּי כִּי

עֵדְוֹתֶיךָ שִׂיחָה לִי ׃ 100 מִזְּקֵנִים אֶתְבּוֹנָן

כִּי פִקּוּדֶיךָ נָצָרְתִּי ׃ 101 מִכָּל־אֹרַח רָע

כָּלִאתִי רַגְלָי לְמַעַן אֶשְׁמֹר דְּבָרֶךָ ׃ 102

50 This is my *a*comfort in my affliction,

That Your word has [1]revived me.

51 The arrogant *a*utterly deride me,

Yet I do not *b*turn aside from Your law.

52 I have *a*remembered Your ordinances from [1]of old, O LORD,

And comfort myself.

53 Burning *a*indignation has seized me because of the wicked,

Who *b*forsake Your law.

54 Your statutes are my songs

In the house of my *a*pilgrimage.

55 O LORD, I *a*remember Your name *b*in the night,

And keep Your law.

56 This has become mine,

[1]That I *a*observe Your precepts.

Psa. 119:57 The LORD is my *a*portion;

I have [1]promised to *b*keep Your words.

58 I *a*sought Your favor *b*with all *my* heart;

*c*Be gracious to me *d*according to Your [1]word.

59 I *a*considered my ways

And turned my feet to Your testimonies.

60 I hastened and did not delay

To keep Your commandments.

61 The *a*cords of the wicked have encircled me,

But I have *b*not forgotten Your law.

62 At *a*midnight I shall rise to give thanks to You

Because of Your *b*righteous ordinances.

מִמִּשְׁפָּטֶיךָ לֹא־סָרְתִּי כִּי־אַתָּה
הוֹרֵתָנִי ׃ 103 מַה־נִּמְלְצוּ לְחִכִּי אִמְרָתֶךָ
מִדְּבַשׁ לְפִי ׃ 104 מִפִּקּוּדֶיךָ אֶתְבּוֹנָן
105 עַל־כֵּן שָׂנֵאתִי ׀ כָּל־אֹרַח שָׁקֶר ׃
106 נֵר־לְרַגְלִי דְבָרֶךָ וְאוֹר לִנְתִיבָתִי ׃
נִשְׁבַּעְתִּי וָאֲקַיֵּמָה לִשְׁמֹר מִשְׁפְּטֵי
צִדְקֶךָ ׃ 107 נַעֲנֵיתִי עַד־מְאֹד יְהֹוָה
חַיֵּנִי כִדְבָרֶךָ ׃ 108 נִדְבוֹת פִּי רְצֵה־נָא
יְהֹוָה וּמִשְׁפָּטֶיךָ לַמְּדֵנִי ׃ 109 נַפְשִׁי
110 בְכַפִּי תָמִיד וְתוֹרָתְךָ לֹא שָׁכָחְתִּי ׃
נָתְנוּ רְשָׁעִים פַּח לִי וּמִפִּקּוּדֶיךָ לֹא
תָעִיתִי ׃ 111 נָחַלְתִּי עֵדְוֹתֶיךָ לְעוֹלָם
כִּי־שְׂשׂוֹן לִבִּי הֵמָּה ׃ 112 נָטִיתִי לִבִּי
לַעֲשׂוֹת חֻקֶּיךָ לְעוֹלָם עֵקֶב ׃ 113 סֵעֲפִים
שָׂנֵאתִי וְתוֹרָתְךָ אָהָבְתִּי ׃ 114 סִתְרִי
וּמָגִנִּי אָתָּה לִדְבָרְךָ יִחָלְתִּי ׃ 115 סוּרוּ־
מִמֶּנִּי מְרֵעִים וְאֶצְּרָה מִצְוֹת אֱלֹהָי ׃ 116
סָמְכֵנִי כְאִמְרָתְךָ וְאֶחְיֶה וְאַל־תְּבִישֵׁנִי
מִשִּׂבְרִי ׃ 117 סְעָדֵנִי וְאִוָּשֵׁעָה וְאֶשְׁעָה
בְחֻקֶּיךָ תָמִיד ׃ 118 סָלִיתָ כָּל־שׁוֹגִים
מֵחֻקֶּיךָ כִּי־שֶׁקֶר תַּרְמִיתָם ׃ 119 סִגִים
הִשְׁבַּתָּ כָל־רִשְׁעֵי־אָרֶץ לָכֵן אָהַבְתִּי
עֵדֹתֶיךָ ׃ 120 סָמַר מִפַּחְדְּךָ בְשָׂרִי
וּמִמִּשְׁפָּטֶיךָ יָרֵאתִי ׃ 121 עָשִׂיתִי מִשְׁפָּט
וָצֶדֶק בַּל־תַּנִּיחֵנִי לְעֹשְׁקָי ׃ 122 עֲרֹב
עַבְדְּךָ לְטוֹב אַל־יַעַשְׁקֻנִי זֵדִים ׃ 123
עֵינַי כָּלוּ לִישׁוּעָתֶךָ וּלְאִמְרַת צִדְקֶךָ ׃
124 עֲשֵׂה עִם־עַבְדְּךָ כְחַסְדֶּךָ וְחֻקֶּיךָ
לַמְּדֵנִי ׃ 125 עַבְדְּךָ־אָנִי הֲבִינֵנִי וְאֵדְעָה
עֵדֹתֶיךָ ׃ 126 עֵת לַעֲשׂוֹת לַיהֹוָה הֵפֵרוּ
תּוֹרָתֶךָ ׃ 127 עַל־כֵּן אָהַבְתִּי מִצְוֹתֶיךָ

63 I am a [a]companion of all those who [1]fear You,

And of those who keep Your precepts.

64 [a]The earth is full of Your lovingkindness, O LORD;

[b]Teach me Your statutes.

Psa. 119:65 You have dealt well with Your servant,

O LORD, according to Your word.

66 Teach me good [1a]discernment and knowledge,

For I believe in Your commandments.

67 [a]Before I was afflicted I went astray,

But now I keep Your word.

68 You are [a]good and [b]do good;

[c]Teach me Your statutes.

69 The arrogant [1]have [a]forged a lie against me;

With all *my* heart I will [b]observe Your precepts.

70 Their heart is [1a]covered with fat,

But I [b]delight in Your law.

71 It is [a]good for me that I was afflicted,

That I may learn Your statutes.

72 The [a]law of Your mouth is better to me

Than thousands of gold and silver *pieces.*

Psa. 119:73 [a]Your hands made me and [1]fashioned me;

[b]Give me understanding, that I may learn Your commandments.

74 May those who [1]fear You [a]see me and be glad,

מִזָּהָב וּמִפָּז ׃ 128 עַל־כֵּן ׀ כָּל־פִּקּוּדֵי

129 כֹל יִשַּׁרְתִּי כָּל־אֹרַח שֶׁקֶר שָׂנֵאתִי ׃

פְּלָאוֹת עֵדְוֹתֶיךָ עַל־כֵּן נְצָרָתַם נַפְשִׁי ׃

130 פֵּתַח דְּבָרֶיךָ יָאִיר מֵבִין פְּתָיִים ׃ 131

פִּי־פָעַרְתִּי וָאֶשְׁאָפָה כִּי לְמִצְוֹתֶיךָ

יָאָבְתִּי ׃ 132 פְּנֵה־אֵלַי וְחָנֵּנִי כְּמִשְׁפָּט

לְאֹהֲבֵי שְׁמֶךָ ׃ 133 פְּעָמַי הָכֵן בְּאִמְרָתֶךָ

וְאַל־תַּשְׁלֶט־בִּי כָל־אָוֶן ׃ 134 פְּדֵנִי

מֵעֹשֶׁק אָדָם וְאֶשְׁמְרָה פִּקּוּדֶיךָ ׃ 135

פָּנֶיךָ הָאֵר בְּעַבְדֶּךָ וְלַמְּדֵנִי אֶת־חֻקֶּיךָ ׃

136 פַּלְגֵי־מַיִם יָרְדוּ עֵינָי עַל לֹא־שָׁמְרוּ

תוֹרָתֶךָ ׃ 137 צַדִּיק אַתָּה יְהוָה וְיָשָׁר

מִשְׁפָּטֶיךָ ׃ 138 צִוִּיתָ צֶדֶק עֵדֹתֶיךָ

וֶאֱמוּנָה מְאֹד ׃ 139 צִמְּתַתְנִי קִנְאָתִי כִּי־

שָׁכְחוּ דְבָרֶיךָ צָרָי ׃ 140 צְרוּפָה

אִמְרָתְךָ מְאֹד וְעַבְדְּךָ אֲהֵבָהּ ׃ 141

צָעִיר אָנֹכִי וְנִבְזֶה פִּקֻּדֶיךָ לֹא שָׁכָחְתִּי ׃

142 צִדְקָתְךָ צֶדֶק לְעוֹלָם וְתוֹרָתְךָ

אֱמֶת ׃ 143 צַר־וּמָצוֹק מְצָאוּנִי מִצְוֹתֶיךָ

שַׁעֲשֻׁעָי ׃ 144 צֶדֶק עֵדְוֹתֶיךָ לְעוֹלָם

הֲבִינֵנִי וְאֶחְיֶה ׃ 145 קָרָאתִי בְכָל־לֵב

עֲנֵנִי יְהוָה חֻקֶּיךָ אֶצֹּרָה ׃ 146 קְרָאתִיךָ

הוֹשִׁיעֵנִי וְאֶשְׁמְרָה עֵדֹתֶיךָ ׃ 147 קִדַּמְתִּי

בַנֶּשֶׁף וָאֲשַׁוֵּעָה לִדְבָרֶיךָ [לְ][דְבָרְךָ]

יִחָלְתִּי ׃ 148 קִדְּמוּ עֵינַי אַשְׁמֻרוֹת לָשִׂיחַ

בְּאִמְרָתֶךָ ׃ 149 קוֹלִי שִׁמְעָה כְחַסְדֶּךָ

יְהוָה כְּמִשְׁפָּטֶךָ חַיֵּנִי ׃ 150 קָרְבוּ רֹדְפֵי

זִמָּה מִתּוֹרָתְךָ רָחָקוּ ׃ 151 קָרוֹב אַתָּה

יְהוָה וְכָל־מִצְוֹתֶיךָ אֱמֶת ׃ 152 קֶדֶם

יָדַעְתִּי מֵעֵדֹתֶיךָ כִּי לְעוֹלָם יְסַדְתָּם ׃

153 רְאֵה־עָנְיִי וְחַלְּצֵנִי כִּי־תוֹרָתְךָ לֹא

Because I [2b]wait for Your word.

75 I know, O LORD, that Your judgments are [a]righteous,

And that [b]in faithfulness You have afflicted me.

76 O may Your lovingkindness [1]comfort me,

According to Your [2]word to Your servant.

77 May [a]Your compassion come to me that I may live,

For Your law is my [b]delight.

78 May [a]the arrogant be ashamed, for they subvert me [b]with a lie;

But I shall [c]meditate on Your precepts.

79 May those who [1]fear You turn to me,

Even those who know Your testimonies.

80 May my heart be [1a]blameless in Your statutes,

So that I will not [b]be ashamed.

Psa. 119:81 My [a]soul languishes for Your salvation;

I [1b]wait for Your word.

82 My [a]eyes fail *with longing* for Your [1]word,

[2]While I say, "When will You comfort me?"

83 Though I have [a]become like a wineskin in the smoke,

I do [b]not forget Your statutes.

84 How many are the [a]days of Your servant?

When will You [b]execute judgment on those who persecute me?

85 The arrogant have [a]dug pits for me,

שְׁכָחְתִּי ׃ 154 רִיבָה רִיבִי וּגְאָלֵנִי
לְאִמְרָתְךָ חַיֵּנִי ׃ 155 רָחוֹק מֵרְשָׁעִים
יְשׁוּעָה כִּי־חֻקֶּיךָ לֹא דָרָשׁוּ ׃ 156
רַחֲמֶיךָ רַבִּים ׀ יְהוָה כְּמִשְׁפָּטֶיךָ חַיֵּנִי ׃
157 רַבִּים רֹדְפַי וְצָרָי מֵעֵדְוֹתֶיךָ לֹא
נָטִיתִי ׃ 158 רָאִיתִי בֹגְדִים וָאֶתְקוֹטָטָה
אֲשֶׁר אִמְרָתְךָ לֹא שָׁמָרוּ ׃ 159 רְאֵה כִּי־
פִקּוּדֶיךָ אָהָבְתִּי יְהוָה כְּחַסְדְּךָ חַיֵּנִי ׃
160 רֹאשׁ־דְּבָרְךָ אֱמֶת וּלְעוֹלָם כָּל־
מִשְׁפַּט צִדְקֶךָ ׃ 161 שָׂרִים רְדָפוּנִי חִנָּם
וּמִדְּבָרֶיךָ [וּ][מִ][דְּבָרְךָ] פָּחַד לִבִּי ׃
162 שָׂשׂ אָנֹכִי עַל־אִמְרָתֶךָ כְּמוֹצֵא שָׁלָל
רָב ׃ 163 שֶׁקֶר שָׂנֵאתִי וַאֲתַעֵבָה תּוֹרָתְךָ
אָהָבְתִּי ׃ 164 שֶׁבַע בַּיּוֹם הִלַּלְתִּיךָ עַל
מִשְׁפְּטֵי צִדְקֶךָ ׃ 165 שָׁלוֹם רָב לְאֹהֲבֵי
תוֹרָתֶךָ וְאֵין־לָמוֹ מִכְשׁוֹל ׃ 166 שִׂבַּרְתִּי
לִישׁוּעָתְךָ יְהוָה וּמִצְוֺתֶיךָ עָשִׂיתִי ׃ 167
שָׁמְרָה נַפְשִׁי עֵדֹתֶיךָ וָאֹהֲבֵם מְאֹד ׃ 168
שָׁמַרְתִּי פִקּוּדֶיךָ וְעֵדֹתֶיךָ כִּי כָל־דְּרָכַי
נֶגְדֶּךָ ׃ 169 תִּקְרַב רִנָּתִי לְפָנֶיךָ יְהוָה
כִּדְבָרְךָ הֲבִינֵנִי ׃ 170 תָּבוֹא תְּחִנָּתִי
לְפָנֶיךָ כְּאִמְרָתְךָ הַצִּילֵנִי ׃ 171 תַּבַּעְנָה
שְׂפָתַי תְּהִלָּה כִּי תְלַמְּדֵנִי חֻקֶּיךָ ׃ 172
תַּעַן לְשׁוֹנִי אִמְרָתֶךָ כִּי כָל־מִצְוֺתֶיךָ
צֶּדֶק ׃ 173 תְּהִי־יָדְךָ לְעָזְרֵנִי כִּי פִקּוּדֶיךָ
בָחָרְתִּי ׃ 174 תָּאַבְתִּי לִישׁוּעָתְךָ יְהוָה
וְתוֹרָתְךָ שַׁעֲשֻׁעָי ׃ 175 תְּחִי־נַפְשִׁי
וּתְהַלְלֶךָּ וּמִשְׁפָּטֶךָ יַעְזְרֻנִי ׃ 176 תָּעִיתִי
כְּשֶׂה אֹבֵד בַּקֵּשׁ עַבְדֶּךָ כִּי מִצְוֺתֶיךָ לֹא
שָׁכָחְתִּי ׃

Men who are not [1]in accord with Your law.

86 All Your commandments are [a]faithful;

They have [b]persecuted me with a lie; [c]help me!

87 They almost destroyed me [1]on earth,

But as for me, I [d]did not forsake Your precepts.

88 Revive me according to Your lovingkindness,

So that I may keep the testimony of Your mouth.

Psa. 119:89 [a]Forever, O LORD,

Your word [1]is settled in heaven.

90 Your [a]faithfulness *continues* [1]throughout all generations;

You [b]established the earth, and it [c]stands.

91 They stand this day according to Your [a]ordinances,

For [b]all things are Your servants.

92 If Your law had not been my [a]delight,

Then I would have perished [b]in my affliction.

93 I will [a]never forget Your precepts,

For by them You have [1b]revived me.

94 I am Yours, [a]save me;

For I have [b]sought Your precepts.

95 The wicked [a]wait for me to destroy me;

I shall diligently consider Your testimonies.

96 I have seen [1]a limit to all perfection;

Your commandment is exceedingly broad.

Psa. 119:97   O how I *a*love Your law!

It is my *b*meditation all the day.

98   Your *a*commandments make me wiser than my enemies,

For they are ever [1]mine.

99   I have more insight than all my teachers,

For Your testimonies are my *a*meditation.

100   I understand *a*more than the aged,

Because I have *b*observed Your precepts.

101   I have *a*restrained my feet from every evil way,

That I may keep Your word.

102   I have not *a*turned aside from Your ordinances,

For You Yourself have taught me.

103   How *a*sweet are Your [1]words to my [2]taste!

Yes, sweeter than honey to my mouth!

104   From Your precepts I *a*get understanding;

Therefore I *b*hate every false way.

Psa. 119:105   Your word is a *a*lamp to my feet

And a light to my path.

106   I have *a*sworn and I will confirm it,

That I will keep Your righteous ordinances.

107   I am exceedingly *a*afflicted;

[1][b]Revive me, O LORD, according to Your word.

108   O accept the *a*freewill offerings of my mouth, O LORD,

And *b*teach me Your ordinances.

109   My [1][a]life is continually [2]in my hand,

Yet I do not [b]forget Your law.

110   The wicked have [a]laid a snare for me,

Yet I have not [b]gone astray from Your precepts.

111   I have [a]inherited Your testimonies forever,

For they are the [b]joy of my heart.

112   I have [a]inclined my heart to perform Your statutes

Forever, *even* [b]to the end.

Psa. 119:113   I hate those who are [a]double-minded,

But I love Your [b]law.

114   You are my [a]hiding place and my [b]shield;

I [1][c]wait for Your word.

115   [a]Depart from me, evildoers,

That I may [b]observe the commandments of my God.

116   [a]Sustain me according to Your [1]word, that I may live;

And [b]do not let me be [2]ashamed of my hope.

117   Uphold me that I may be [a]safe,

That I may [b]have regard for Your statutes continually.

118   You have [1]rejected all those [a]who wander from Your statutes,

For their deceitfulness is [2]useless.

119   You have [1]removed all the wicked of the earth *like* [a]dross;

Therefore I [b]love Your testimonies.

120   My flesh [1][a]trembles for fear of You,

And I am [b]afraid of Your judgments.

Psa. 119:121   I have *a*done justice and righteousness;

Do not leave me to my oppressors.

122   Be *a*surety for Your servant for good;

Do not let the arrogant *b*oppress me.

123   My *a*eyes fail *with longing* for Your salvation

And for Your righteous [1]word.

124   Deal with Your servant *a*according to Your lovingkindness

And *b*teach me Your statutes.

125   *a*I am Your servant; *b*give me understanding,

That I may know Your testimonies.

126   It is time for the LORD to *a*act,

For they have broken Your law.

127   Therefore I *a*love Your commandments

Above gold, yes, above fine gold.

128   Therefore I esteem right all *Your* *a*precepts concerning everything,

I *b*hate every false way.

Psa. 119:129   Your testimonies are *a*wonderful;

Therefore my soul *b*observes them.

130   The *a*unfolding of Your words gives light;

It gives *b*understanding to the simple.

131   I *a*opened my mouth wide and *b*panted,

For I *a*longed for Your commandments.

132   *a*Turn to me and be gracious to me,

After Your manner [1]with those who love Your name.

133 Establish my [a]footsteps in Your [1]word,

And do not let any iniquity [b]have dominion over me.

134 [a]Redeem me from the oppression of man,

That I may keep Your precepts.

135 [a]Make Your face shine upon Your servant,

And [b]teach me Your statutes.

136 My eyes [1]shed [a]streams of water,

Because they [b]do not keep Your law.

Psa. 119:137 [a]Righteous are You, O LORD,

And upright are Your judgments.

138 You have commanded Your testimonies in [a]righteousness

And exceeding [b]faithfulness.

139 My [a]zeal has [1]consumed me,

Because my adversaries have forgotten Your words.

140 Your [1a]word is very [2]pure,

Therefore Your servant [b]loves it.

141 I am small and [a]despised,

Yet I do not [b]forget Your precepts.

142 Your righteousness is an everlasting righteousness,

And [a]Your law is truth.

143 Trouble and anguish have [1]come upon me,

Yet Your commandments are my [a]delight.

144 Your [a]testimonies are righteous forever;

[b]Give me understanding that I may live.

Psa. 119:145 I cried [a]with all my heart; answer me, O LORD!

<table>
<tr><td>

I will *b*observe Your statutes.

146   I cried to You; *a*save me

And I shall keep Your testimonies.

147   I [1]*a*rise before dawn and cry for help;

I [2]wait for Your words.

148   My eyes anticipate the *a*night watches,

That I may *b*meditate on Your [1]word.

149   Hear my voice *a*according to Your lovingkindness;

*b*Revive me, O LORD, according to Your ordinances.

150   Those who follow after wickedness draw near;

They are far from Your law.

151   You are *a*near, O LORD,

And all Your commandments are *b*truth.

152   Of old I have *a*known from Your testimonies

That You have founded them *b*forever.

Psa. 119:153   *a*Look upon my *b*affliction and rescue me,

For I do not *c*forget Your law.

154   *a*Plead my cause and *b*redeem me;

Revive me according to Your [1]word.

155   Salvation is *a*far from the wicked,

For they *b*do not seek Your statutes.

156   [1]*a*Great are Your mercies, O LORD;

Revive me according to Your ordinances.

157   Many are my *a*persecutors and my adversaries,

</td><td></td></tr>
</table>

Yet I do not [b]turn aside from Your testimonies.

158 I behold the [a]treacherous and [b]loathe *them,*

Because they do not keep Your [1]word.

159 Consider how I [a]love Your precepts;

[b]Revive me, O LORD, according to Your lovingkindness.

160 The [a]sum of Your word is [b]truth,

And every one of Your righteous ordinances [c]is everlasting.

Psa. 119:161 [a]Princes persecute me without cause,

But my heart [b]stands in awe of Your words.

162 I [a]rejoice at Your [1]word,

As one who [b]finds great spoil.

163 I [a]hate and despise falsehood,

But I [b]love Your law.

164 Seven times a day I praise You,

Because of Your [a]righteous ordinances.

165 Those who love Your law have [a]great peace,

And [1b]nothing causes them to stumble.

166 I [a]hope for Your salvation, O LORD,

And do Your commandments.

167 My [a]soul keeps Your testimonies,

And I [b]love them exceedingly.

168 I [a]keep Your precepts and Your testimonies,

For all my [b]ways are before You.

Psa. 119:169 Let my [a]cry [1]come before You, O LORD;

[b]Give me understanding [c]according to Your word.

170 Let my [a]supplication come before You;

[b]Deliver me according to Your [1]word.

171 Let my [a]lips utter praise,

For You [b]teach me Your statutes.

172 Let my [a]tongue sing of Your [1]word,

For all Your [b]commandments are righteousness.

173 Let Your [a]hand be [1]ready to help me,

For I have [b]chosen Your precepts.

174 I [a]long for Your salvation, O LORD,

And Your law is my [b]delight.

175 Let my [a]soul live that it may praise You,

And let Your ordinances help me.

176 I have [a]gone astray like a lost sheep; seek Your servant,

For I do [b]not forget Your commandments.

References

Psalm 119:1
[1]Lit *complete;* or *having integrity*
[a]Ps 101:2, 6; Prov 11:20; 13:6
[b]Ps 128:1; Ezek 11:20; 18:17; Mic 4:2

Psalm 119:2
[a]Ps 25:10; 99:7; 119:22, 168
[b]Deut 4:29; Ps 119:10
[c]Deut 6:5; 10:12; 11:13; 13:3; 30:2

Psalm 119:3
[a]1 John 3:9; 5:18

Psalm 119:4
[1]Lit *commanded*
[2]Lit *To keep*
[a]Deut 4:13; Neh 9:13

Psalm 119:5
[a]Ps 40:2; Prov 4:26
[b]Deut 12:1; 2 Chr 7:17

Psalm 119:6
[1]Lit *to*
[a]Job 22:26; Ps 119:80

Psalm 119:7
[a]Ps 119:62

Psalm 119:8
[a]Ps 38:21; 71:9, 18

Psalm 119:9
[a]1 Kin 2:4; 8:25; 2 Chr 6:16

Psalm 119:10
[a]2 Chr 15:15; Ps 119:2, 145
[b]Ps 119:21, 118

Psalm 119:11
*a*Ps 37:31; 40:8; Luke 2:19, 51

Psalm 119:12
*a*Ps 119:26, 64, 108, 124, 135, 171

Psalm 119:13
*a*Ps 40:9
*b*Ps 119:72

Psalm 119:14
[1]Lit *As over all*
*a*Ps 119:111, 162

Psalm 119:15
[1]Or *look upon*
*a*Ps 1:2; 119:23, 48, 78, 97, 148
*b*Ps 25:4; 27:11; Is 58:2

Psalm 119:16
[1]Lit *delight myself*
*a*Ps 1:2; 119:24, 35, 47, 70, 77, 92, 143, 174
*b*Ps 119:93

Psalm 119:17
*a*Ps 13:6; 116:7

Psalm 119:19
*a*Gen 47:9; Lev 25:23; 1 Chr 29:15; Ps 39:12; 119:54; Heb 11:13

Psalm 119:20
[1]Lit *for*
*a*Ps 42:1, 2; 63:1; 84:2; 119:40, 131

Psalm 119:21
[1]Or *Cursed are those who wander...*
*a*Ps 68:30
*b*Deut 27:26; Ps 37:22
*c*Ps 119:10, 118

Psalm 119:22

[a]Ps 39:8; 119:39
[b]Ps 119:2

Psalm 119:23
[a]Ps 119:161
[b]Ps 119:15

Psalm 119:24
[1]Lit *the men of my counsel*
[a]Ps 119:16

Psalm 119:25
[a]Ps 44:25
[b]Ps 119:37, 40, 88, 93, 107, 149, 154, 156, 159; 143:11
[c]Ps 119:65

Psalm 119:26
[a]Ps 25:4; 27:11; 86:11; 119:12

Psalm 119:27
[a]Ps 105:2; 145:5

Psalm 119:28
[1]Lit *drops*
[a]Ps 22:14; 107:26
[b]Ps 20:2; 1 Pet 5:10

Psalm 119:30
[1]Or *accounted Your ordinances worthy*

Psalm 119:31
[a]Deut 11:22

Psalm 119:32
[a]1 Kin 4:29; Is 60:5; 2 Cor 6:11, 13

Psalm 119:33
[a]Ps 119:5, 12

Psalm 119:34
[a]Ps 119:27, 73, 125, 144, 169

[b]1 Chr 22:12; Ezek 44:24
[c]Ps 119:2, 69

Psalm 119:35
[a]Ps 25:4; Is 40:14
[b]Ps 112:1; 119:16

Psalm 119:36
[a]1 Kin 8:58
[b]Ezek 33:31; Mark 7:21, 22; Luke 12:15; Heb 13:5

Psalm 119:37
[a]Is 33:15
[b]Ps 71:20; 119:25

Psalm 119:38
[1]Or *promise*
[2]Lit *Which is for the fear of You*
[a]2 Sam 7:25

Psalm 119:39
[a]Ps 119:22

Psalm 119:40
[a]Ps 119:20

Psalm 119:41
[1]Or *promise*
[a]Ps 119:77
[b]Ps 119:58, 76, 116, 170

Psalm 119:42
[a]Prov 27:11
[b]Ps 102:8; 119:39

Psalm 119:43
[1]Or *hope in*
[a]Ps 119:49, 74, 81, 114, 147

Psalm 119:44
[b]Ps 119:33

Psalm 119:45
[1]Lit *in a wide place*
[a]Prov 4:12
[b]Ps 119:94, 155

Psalm 119:46
[a]Matt 10:18; Acts 26:1, 2

Psalm 119:47
[1]Lit *delight myself*
[a]Ps 119:16
[b]Ps 119:97, 127, 159

Psalm 119:48
[a]Ps 119:97, 127, 159
[b]Ps 119:15

Psalm 119:49
[1]Lit *On*

Psalm 119:50
[1]Or *preserved me alive*
[a]Job 6:10; Rom 15:4

Psalm 119:51
[a]Job 30:1; Jer 20:7
[b]Job 23:11; Ps 44:18; 119:157

Psalm 119:52
[1]Or *everlasting*
[a]Ps 103:18

Psalm 119:53
[a]Ex 32:19; Ezra 9:3; Neh 13:25; Ps 119:158
[b]Ps 89:30

Psalm 119:54
[a]Gen 47:9; Ps 119:19

Psalm 119:55

[a]Ps 63:6
[b]Ps 42:8; 92:2; 119:62; Is 26:9; Acts 16:25

Psalm 119:56
[1]Or *Because*
[a]Ps 119:22, 69, 100

Psalm 119:57
[1]Lit *said that I would keep*
[a]Ps 16:5; Lam 3:24
[b]Deut 33:9

Psalm 119:58
[1]Or *promise*
[a]1 Kin 13:6
[b]Ps 119:2
[c]Ps 41:4; 56:1; 57:1
[d]Ps 119:41

Psalm 119:59
[a]Mark 14:72; Luke 15:17

Psalm 119:61
[a]Job 36:8; Ps 140:5
[b]Ps 119:83, 141, 153, 176

Psalm 119:62
[a]Ps 119:55
[b]Ps 119:7

Psalm 119:63
[1]Or *revere*
[a]Ps 101:6

Psalm 119:64
[a]Ps 33:5
[b]Ps 119:12

Psalm 119:66
[1]Or *judgment*
[a]Phil 1:9

Psalm 119:67
[a]Ps 119:71, 75; Jer 31:18, 19; Heb 12:5-11

Psalm 119:68
[a]Ps 86:5; 100:5; 106:1; 107:1; Matt 19:17
[b]Deut 8:16; 28:63; 30:5; Ps 125:4
[c]Ps 119:12

Psalm 119:69
[1]Lit *besmear me with lies*
[a]Job 13:4; Ps 109:2
[b]Ps 119:56

Psalm 119:70
[1]Lit *gross like fat*
[a]Deut 32:15; Job 15:27; Ps 17:10; Is 6:10; Jer 5:28; Acts 28:27
[b]Ps 119:16

Psalm 119:71
[a]Ps 119:67, 75

Psalm 119:72
[a]Ps 19:10; 119:127; Prov 8:10, 11, 19

Psalm 119:73
[1]Lit *established*
[a]Job 10:8; 31:15; Ps 100:3; 138:8; 139:15, 16
[b]Ps 119:34

Psalm 119:74
[1]Or *revere*
[2]Or *hope in*
[a]Ps 34:2; 35:27; 107:42
[b]Ps 119:43

Psalm 119:75
[a]Ps 119:138
[b]Heb 12:10

Psalm 119:76

[1]Lit *be for my comfort*
[2]Or *promise*

Psalm 119:77
[a]Ps 119:41
[b]Ps 119:16

Psalm 119:78
[a]Jer 50:32
[b]Ps 119:86
[c]Ps 119:15

Psalm 119:79
[1]Or *revere*

Psalm 119:80
[1]Lit *complete;* or *having integrity*
[a]Ps 119:1
[b]Ps 119:46

Psalm 119:81
[1]Or *hope in*
[a]Ps 84:2
[b]Ps 119:43

Psalm 119:82
[1]Or *promise*
[2]Lit *Saying*
[a]Ps 69:3; 119:123; Is 38:14; Lam 2:11

Psalm 119:83
[a]Job 30:30
[b]Ps 119:61

Psalm 119:84
[a]Ps 39:4
[b]Rev 6:10

Psalm 119:85
[1]Lit *according to Your law*
[a]Ps 7:15; 35:7; 57:6; Jer 18:22

Psalm 119:86
[a]Ps 119:138
[b]Ps 35:19; 119:78, 161
[c]Ps 109:26

Psalm 119:87
[1]Lit *in the earth*
[a]Is 58:2

Psalm 119:89
[1]Lit *stands firm*
[a]Ps 89:2; 119:160; Is 40:8; Matt 24:35; 1 Pet 1:25

Psalm 119:90
[1]Lit *to*
[a]Ps 36:5; 89:1, 2
[b]Ps 148:6
[c]Eccl 1:4

Psalm 119:91
[a]Jer 31:35; 33:25
[b]Ps 104:2-4

Psalm 119:92
[a]Ps 119:16
[b]Ps 119:50

Psalm 119:93
[1]Or *kept me alive*
[a]Ps 119:16, 83
[b]Ps 119:25

Psalm 119:94
[a]Ps 119:146
[b]Ps 119:45

Psalm 119:95
[a]Ps 40:14; Is 32:7

Psalm 119:96

[1]Lit *an end of*

Psalm 119:97
[a]Ps 119:47, 48, 127, 163, 165
[b]Ps 1:2; 119:15

Psalm 119:98
[1]Or *with me*
[a]Deut 4:6; Ps 119:130

Psalm 119:99
[a]Ps 119:15

Psalm 119:100
[a]Job 32:7-9
[b]Ps 119:22, 56

Psalm 119:101
[a]Prov 1:15

Psalm 119:102
[a]Deut 17:20; Josh 23:6; 1 Kin 15:5

Psalm 119:103
[1]Or *promises*
[2]Lit *palate*
[a]Ps 19:10; Prov 8:11; 24:13, 14

Psalm 119:104
[a]Ps 119:130
[b]Ps 119:128

Psalm 119:105
[a]Prov 6:23

Psalm 119:106
[a]Neh 10:29

Psalm 119:107
[1]Or *Keep me alive*
[a]Ps 119:25, 50

[b]Ps 119:25

Psalm 119:108
[a]Hos 14:2; Heb 13:15
[b]Ps 119:12

Psalm 119:109
[1]Lit *soul*
[2]I.e. in danger
[a]Judg 12:3; Job 13:14
[b]Ps 119:16

Psalm 119:110
[a]Ps 91:3; 140:5; 141:9
[b]Ps 119:10

Psalm 119:111
[a]Deut 33:4
[b]Ps 119:14, 162

Psalm 119:112
[a]Ps 119:36
[b]Ps 119:33

Psalm 119:113
[a]1 Kin 18:21; James 1:8; 4:8
[b]Ps 119:47

Psalm 119:114
[1]Or *hope in*
[a]Ps 31:20; 32:7; 61:4; 91:1
[b]Ps 84:9
[c]Ps 119:74

Psalm 119:115
[a]Ps 6:8; 139:19; Matt 7:23
[b]Ps 119:22

Psalm 119:116
[1]Or *promise*
[2]Lit *put to shame because of*

*a*Ps 37:17, 24; 54:4
*b*Ps 25:2, 20; 31:1, 17; Rom 5:5; 9:33; Phil 1:20

Psalm 119:117
*a*Ps 12:5; Prov 29:25
*b*Ps 119:6, 15

Psalm 119:118
[1]Lit *made light of*
[2]Lit *falsehood*
*a*Ps 119:10, 21

Psalm 119:119
[1]Lit *caused to cease*
*a*Is 1:22, 25; Ezek 22:18, 19
*b*Ps 119:47

Psalm 119:120
[1]Lit *bristles up from*
*a*Job 4:14; Hab 3:16
*b*Ps 119:161

Psalm 119:121
*a*2 Sam 8:15; Job 29:14

Psalm 119:122
*a*Job 17:3; Heb 7:22
*b*Ps 119:134

Psalm 119:123
[1]Or *promise*
*a*Ps 119:82

Psalm 119:124
*a*Ps 51:1; 106:45; 109:26; 119:88, 149, 159
*b*Ps 119:12

Psalm 119:125
*a*Ps 116:16
*b*Ps 119:27

Psalm 119:126
*^a*Jer 18:23; Ezek 31:11

Psalm 119:127
*^a*Ps 19:10; 119:47

Psalm 119:128
*^a*Ps 19:8
*^b*Ps 119:104

Psalm 119:129
*^a*Ps 119:18
*^b*Ps 119:22

Psalm 119:130
*^a*Prov 6:23
*^b*Ps 19:7

Psalm 119:131
*^a*Job 29:23; Ps 81:10
*^b*Ps 42:1
*^c*Ps 119:20

Psalm 119:132
[1]Lit *to*
*^a*Ps 25:16; 106:4

Psalm 119:133
[1]Or *promise*
*^a*Ps 17:5
*^b*Ps 19:13; Rom 6:12

Psalm 119:134
*^a*Ps 119:84; 142:6; Luke 1:74

Psalm 119:135
*^a*Num 6:25; Ps 4:6; 31:16; 67:1; 80:3, 7, 19
*^b*Ps 119:12

Psalm 119:136
[1]Lit *run down*

[a]Jer 9:1, 18; 14:17; Lam 3:48
[b]Ps 119:158

Psalm 119:137
[a]Ezra 9:15; Neh 9:33; Ps 116:5; 129:4; 145:17; Jer 12:1; Lam 1:18; Dan 9:7, 14

Psalm 119:138
[a]Ps 19:7-9; 119:144, 172
[b]Ps 119:86, 90

Psalm 119:139
[1]Lit *put an end to*
[a]Ps 69:9; John 2:17

Psalm 119:140
[1]Or *promise*
[2]Lit *refined*
[a]Ps 12:6; 19:8
[b]Ps 119:47

Psalm 119:141
[a]Ps 22:6
[b]Ps 119:61

Psalm 119:142
[a]Ps 19:9; 119:151, 160

Psalm 119:143
[1]Lit *found me*
[a]Ps 119:24

Psalm 119:144
[a]Ps 19:9
[b]Ps 119:27

Psalm 119:145
[a]Ps 119:10
[b]Ps 119:22, 55

Psalm 119:146
[a]Ps 3:7

Psalm 119:147
[1]Lit *anticipate the dawn*
[2]Or *hope in*
[a]Ps 5:3; 57:8; 108:2

Psalm 119:148
[1]Or *promise*
[a]Ps 63:6
[b]Ps 119:15

Psalm 119:149
[a]Ps 119:124
[b]Ps 119:25

Psalm 119:151
[a]Ps 34:18; 145:18; Is 50:8
[b]Ps 119:142

Psalm 119:152
[a]Ps 119:125
[b]Ps 119:89; Luke 21:33

Psalm 119:153
[a]Lam 5:1
[b]Ps 119:50
[c]Ps 119:16; Prov 3:1; Hos 4:6

Psalm 119:154
[1]Or *promise*
[a]1 Sam 24:15; Ps 35:1; Mic 7:9
[b]Ps 119:134

Psalm 119:155
[a]Job 5:4
[b]Ps 119:45, 94

Psalm 119:156
[1]Or *Many*
[a]2 Sam 24:14

Psalm 119:157
*a*Ps 7:1; 119:86, 161
*b*Ps 119:51

Psalm 119:158
[1]Or *promise*
*a*Is 21:2; 24:16
*b*Ps 139:21

Psalm 119:159
*a*Ps 119:47
*b*Ps 119:25

Psalm 119:160
*a*Ps 139:17
*b*Ps 119:142
*c*Ps 119:89, 152

Psalm 119:161
*a*1 Sam 24:11; 26:18; Ps 119:23
*b*Ps 119:120

Psalm 119:162
[1]Or *promise*
*a*Ps 119:14, 111
*b*1 Sam 30:16; Is 9:3

Psalm 119:163
*a*Ps 31:6; 119:104, 128; Prov 13:5
*b*Ps 119:47

Psalm 119:164
*a*Ps 119:7, 160

Psalm 119:165
[1]Lit *they have no stumbling block*
*a*Ps 37:11; Prov 3:2; Is 26:3; 32:17
*b*Prov 3:23; Is 63:13; 1 John 2:10

Psalm 119:166
*a*Gen 49:18; Ps 119:81, 174

Psalm 119:167
*a*Ps 119:129
*b*Ps 119:47

Psalm 119:168
*a*Ps 119:22
*b*Job 24:23; Ps 139:3; Prov 5:21

Psalm 119:169
[1]Lit *come near before*
*a*Job 16:18; Ps 18:6; 102:1
*b*Ps 119:27, 144
*c*Ps 119:65, 154

Psalm 119:170
[1]Or *promise*
*a*Ps 28:2; 130:2; 140:6; 143:1
*b*Ps 22:20; 31:2; 59:1

Psalm 119:171
*a*Ps 51:15; 63:3
*b*Ps 94:12; 119:12; Is 2:3; Mic 4:2

Psalm 119:172
[1]Or *promise*
*a*Ps 51:14
*b*Ps 119:138

Psalm 119:173
[1]Lit *to help me*
*a*Ps 37:24; 73:23
*b*Josh 24:22; Luke 10:42

Psalm 119:174
*a*Ps 119:166
*b*Ps 119:16, 24

Psalm 119:175
*a*Is 55:3

Psalm 119:176
[a]Is 53:6; Jer 50:6; Matt 18:12; Luke 15:4
[b]Ps 119:16

Targum

Psa. 119:1 How happy are the perfect of way, who walk in the Torah of the LORD. ² How happy those who keep his testimony; with a whole heart they will seek his instruction. ³ Truly, they have not acted deceitfully; in his proper ways they have walked. ⁴ You have given your commandments, to keep very much. ⁵ It is good for me that my ways are straight, to keep your decrees. ⁶ Then I will not be disappointed when I look to all your commandments. ⁷ I will give thanks in your presence with uprightness of heart, when I learn the judgments of your righteousness. ⁸ I will keep your decrees; do not abandon me utterly. ⁹ In what way shall a youth purify his way? To keep [it] as your words. ¹⁰ With all my heart I have sought your teaching; do not let me go astray from your commandments. ¹¹ In my heart I have hidden your word, that I might not sin in your presence. ¹² Blessed are you, O LORD; teach me your decrees. ¹³ With my lips I have recounted all the judgments of your mouth. ¹⁴ In the way of your testimonies I have rejoiced, as at a stroke of luck. ¹⁵ I will speak by your commandments, and I will behold, your ways. ¹⁶ I will find delight in your decrees, I will not forget your utterance. ¹⁷ Requite your servant with good; I will live, and keep your words. ¹⁸ Uncover my eyes, and I will behold, wonders from your Torah. ¹⁹ I am a dweller in the land; do not take away your commandments from me. ²⁰ My soul has longed with longing for your commandments at all times. ²¹ You have rebuked the malicious; cursed are all who stray from your commandments. ²² Remove from me humiliation and shame; for I have kept your testimonies. ²³ For leaders sit speaking against me; your servant is engaged in instruction of your decrees. ²⁴ Also your testimonies are my delight, the source of my counsel. ²⁵ My soul is joined to the dust; heal me according to your word. ²⁶ I numbered my ways and you received my prayer; teach me your decrees. ²⁷ Give me insight into the way of your commandments, and I will speak of your wonders. ²⁸ My soul is grieved by weariness; sustain me according to your word. ²⁹ Remove from me the path of lies; and [by] your Torah have compassion on me. ³⁰ I have chosen the faithful path; I have placed your judgements [with me]. ³¹ I have joined myself to your testimonies, O LORD; do not make me ashamed. ³² I will run in the path of your commandments, for you will expand my heart. ³³ Teach me, O LORD, the way of your decrees, and I will keep it totally. ³⁴ Give me insight, and I will keep your Torah, O LORD; and I will keep it with a whole heart. ³⁵ Make me walk in the course of your commandments, for I desire it. ³⁶ Incline my heart to your testimonies, and not to money. ³⁷ Turn my eyes away from the sight of deceit; by your words heal me. ³⁸ Confirm your word to your servant, which [leads] to your worship. ³⁹ Take away my reproach, which I fear, for your judgments are good. ⁴⁰ Behold, I have yearned for your commandments; in your generosity heal me. ⁴¹ And let your kindness come upon me, O LORD, your redemption in accordance with your word. **42** And I will give answer to those who mock me, for I have trusted in your word. **43** And do not remove the word of truth from my mouth utterly, for I have waited long for your judgments. **44** And I will keep your Torah always, for ages upon ages. **45** And I will walk in the wideness of the Torah, for I have sought your commandments. **46** And I will speak of your testimonies before kings, and I will not be ashamed. **47** And I will delight myself in your commandments, which I love. **48** And I will lift my hands to your commandments, which I love, and I will speak of your decrees. **49** Remind your servant of the word, for you waited long for me. **50** This is my comfort in my pain, for your word has sustained me. **51** The malicious mock me greatly; I have not turned away from your Torah. **52** I remembered your judgments of old, O LORD, and I was comforted. **53** Trembling seized me because of the wicked who forsake your Torah. **54** Your decrees became psalms for me in my dwelling place. **55** I remembered your name in the night, O LORD, and I kept your Torah. **56** This became merit for me, for I kept your commandments. **57** My portion is the LORD, I have promised to keep your words. **58** I have prayed in your presence with a whole heart; have pity on me according to your word. **59** I have thought to improve my way, and I will turn my feet to your testimonies. **60** I was eager, and did not delay to keep your commandments. **61** The band of wicked men has gathered against me; I have not forgotten your Torah. **62** In the middle of the night I will rise to sing praise in your presence, for the sake of your righteous judgments. **63** I am a companion to all who revere you, and to those who keep your commandments. **64** Your goodness, O LORD, fills the earth; teach me your decrees. **65** You have shown goodness to your servant, O LORD, according to your words. **66** Teach me good sense and knowledge, for I have believed in your commandments. **67** Before I was afflicted, I was in error, but now I have kept your word. **68** You are good, and do good; teach me your decrees. **69** The malicious have shouted me down with lies; I will keep your commandments with a whole heart. **70** The impulse of their heart is dulled as with fat; as for me, my delight is your Torah. **71** It is good for me, for I was humbled, so that I might learn your decrees. **72** Better for me is the Torah of your mouth, than a thousand talents of gold and silver. **73** Your hands made me and established me; give me insight and I will learn your commandments. **74** Those who fear you will see me and be glad; for I have waited long for your word. **75** I know, O LORD, for your judgments are righteous and you have afflicted me in truth. **76** Now let your kindness be for my comfort, according to your word to your servant. **77** Let your mercies come to me and I will live; for your Torah is my delight. **78** The arrogant will be ashamed, for they twisted a lie against me; I will speak of your commandments. **79** Those who fear you will turn to my teaching, and those who know your testimonies. **80** Let my heart be without blemish in your decrees, so that I may not be ashamed. **81** My soul has yearned for your redemption; I have waited long for your word. [82] My eyes are spent for your word, saying, "When will you comfort me?" [83] For I have become like a water-skin that hangs in the smoke; your decrees I have not forgotten. [84] How many are the days of your servant? When will you pass judgment on my persecutors? [85] The malicious have dug pits for me, that you have not commanded them in your Torah. [86] All your commandments are truth; for a lie they persecuted me, help me! [87] They almost destroyed me in the land; but I have not forsaken your commandments. [88] Sustain me according to your kindness, and I will keep the testimony of your mouth. [89] Forever, O LORD, your word endures in heaven. [90] Your faithfulness is to every generation; you established the earth and it endures. [91] This day have they risen for your judgments, for all of them are your servants. [92] Had your Torah not been my delight, then I would have perished in my affliction. [93] I will never forget your commandments, for you have sustained me by them. [94] For I am yours, redeem me; for I have sought after your commandments. [95] The wicked waited for me to annihilate me; I will contemplate your commandments. [96] To everything that began and ended I have seen an end; your commands are very spacious. [97] How I have loved your Torah! It is my conversation all day. [98] Your commandments make me wiser than my enemies; because it is always mine. [99] I have understood more than all my teachers; for your testimonies are my conversation. [100] I will have greater insight than the wise, for I have kept your commandments. [101] I have kept my feet from every evil way, so that I may keep your words. [102] I have not gone away from your judgments, for you have taught me. [103] How sweet to my palate are your words; sweeter by far than honey to my mouth. [104] I will gain insight from your commandments; because of this, I hate every son of man who lies. [105] Your words are like a lamp that illuminates my feet, and a light for my path. [106] I have sworn and covenanted to keep the commandments of your righteousness. [107] I was greatly afflicted, O LORD; heal me according to your words. [108] Be pleased now, O LORD, with the offerings of my mouth; and teach me your judgments. [109] My soul is always in danger by my own hands; but I have not forgotten your Torah. [110] The wicked have arranged a trap for me; but I have not strayed from your commandments. [111] I have inherited your testimonies forever; for they are the joy of my heart. [112] I have inclined my heart to do your decrees forever, to the very end. [113] I hate those who think vain thoughts, but I have loved your Torah. [114] You are my hiding place and my shield; I have waited long for your word. [115] Turn from me, evildoers; and I will keep the commandments of my God. [116] Support me by your word, and I will live; and do not disappoint me because of my trust. [117] Help me and I will be redeemed; and I will be happy in your Torah always. [118] You have subdued all who went astray from your decrees; for their deceit is a lie. [119] You have terminated all the unfit, you have frustrated all the wicked of the earth; because of this, I have loved your testimonies. [120] My flesh is blushing for fear of you; and I am afraid of your judgments.

[121] I have practiced justice and righteousness; do not abandon me to my oppressors. [122] Delight your servant with goodness; do not let the malicious oppress me. [123] My eyes have hoped for your redemption, and for the word of your righteousness. [124] Act with your servant according to your kindness, and teach me your decrees. [125] I am your servant, give me insight, and I will know your testimonies. [126] It is time to do the will of the LORD; the scholars have desecrated your Torah. [127] Because of this, I have loved your commandments more than gold and more than pure gold. [128] Because of this, I have harmonized all the commandments whatsoever; I hate every way of deceit. [129] Your testimonies are wonderful; because of this, my soul has kept them. [130] Your engraved words will enlighten the needy, the simple will gain insight. [131] I opened my mouth and learned, for I desired your commandments. [132] Turn to me and have compassion on me, as is the custom towards those who love your name. [133] Establish my steps by your word, and let no deceit rule over me. [134] Redeem me from the oppression of the son of man, and I will keep your commandments. [135] Shine the splendor of your face on your servant, and teach me your decrees. [136] Streams of water will go down my eyes, because they have not kept the Torah. [137] Your are righteous, O LORD, and your judgments are upright. [138] You have commanded righteousness, testimony, and much faithfulness. [139] My zeal has overcome me, for my oppressors have forgotten your words. [140] Your word is very pure, and your servant loves it. [141] I am small and despised; I have not forgotten your commandments. [142] Your generosity is righteousness forever, and your Torah is truth. [143] Trouble and the oppressor have befallen me; your commandments are my delight. [144] Your testimonies are righteousness forever; give me insight and I will endure. [145] I have called with a whole heart; answer me, O LORD! I will keep your decrees. [146] I have called you, redeem me; and I will keep your testimonies. [147] I have risen early at dawn, and prayed; I have waited long for your word. [148] My eyes have preceded the watches of morning and evening to speak of your word. [149] Hear my voice in accordance with your kindness, O LORD; sustain me according to your judgments. [150] Those who pursue fornication have drawn near; they have gone far from your Torah. [151] You are near, O LORD, and all your commandments are truth. [152] Long ago I grew wise from your testimonies, for you founded them forever. [153] See my affliction and deliver me; for I have not forgotten your Torah. [154] Argue my case and redeem me; heal me for your word. [155] Redemption is far from the wicked; for they have not sought your decrees. [156] Your mercies are many, O LORD; heal me according to your judgments. [157] Those who pursue me and oppress me are many; I have not turned away from your testimonies. [158] I saw despoilers and I contended with them, who have not kept your word. [159] See [this], for I have loved your commandments; O LORD, according to your kindness heal me. [160] The beginning of your word is truth; and all the judgments of your righteousness are forever. [161] Rulers have pursued me

without cause; and my heart is in fear of your word. [162] I am glad concerning your word, like a man who finds much spoil. [163] I have hated deceit and loathed it; I have loved your Torah. [164] Seven times a day I have praised you, because of the judgements of your righteousness. [165] There is great peace for those who love your Torah in this age, and they have no stumbling-block in the age to come. [166] I have hoped for your redemption, O LORD, and I have done your commandments. [167] My soul has kept your testimonies, and I have loved them greatly. [168] I have kept your commandments and your testimonies, for all my ways are before you. [169] My prayer will come near in your presence, O LORD; give me insight according to your word. [170] Let my prayer come before you; deliver me according to your word. [171] My lips will seek praise, for you will teach me your decrees. [172] My tongue will reply [to] your word, for all your judgments are righteousness. [173] May your hand be [ready] to help me, for I have taken pleasure in your commandments. [174] I have yearned for your redemption, O LORD, and your Torah is my delight. [175] May my soul live and praise you, and may your judgments give me aid. [176] I have gone astray like a lost flock; seek your servant, for I have not forgotten your commandments.

Spiritual Awareness

Introduction

This Psalm outlines the life of King David. He was always attempting to reach self-perfection in his service to the LORD. Every step he took was to bring him closer to the LORD. He made a few missteps along the way. This Psalm follows the sequence of the Hebrew alphabet as it describes his life. David described the many obstacles and dangers that confronted him during his lifetime. Even in times of sorrow, he never lost his faith nor his objective.

Notes of the Psalm

This entire psalm is a lesson in spiritual awareness. How many people today attempt to reach the LORD throughout their lives? David made it a top priority. Ask yourself, where does the LORD come into play in your life? Unfortunately, the major mechanism to help people find the LORD are man-made institutions. These institutions are more concerned about their survival rather than the survival of the membership. Politics and power are the mainstay in churches and synagogues.

How can a person find their spirituality when the institutions originally designed to help are now corrupt? This is where self-study of the Bible is necessary. There are many biblical researchers on the internet. Beware of many and check out their credentials and writings. In Hebraic studies, there are many ways to express an interpretation of the Bible. Rabbi Steinsaltz said that every person needs to put together their own Torah. He meant that there are numerous ways to understand the LORD's words. If your interpretation is not anti-biblical, it is acceptable as your view.

There is a church denomination today (2023) in which its leadership, the bishops, says that the Bible is just a book of ancient stories. In addition, they espouse that the Bible does not have to be followed. If they toss the Bible out of this church, then it is no longer a church but a large social club. So, if you are a part of a religious organization, ensure that it follows the LORD's word.

Psalm 120

New American Standard 1995	Hebrew
Psa. 120:0 A Song of [†]Ascents. **Psa. 120:1** [a]In my trouble I cried to the LORD, 　　And He answered me. 2　　Deliver my soul, O LORD, from [a]lying lips, 　　From a [b]deceitful tongue. 3　　What shall be given to you, and what more shall be done to you, 　　You [a]deceitful tongue? 4　　[a]Sharp arrows of the warrior, 　　With the *burning* [b]coals of the broom tree. **Psa. 120:5** Woe is me, for I sojourn in [a]Meshech, 　　For I dwell among the [b]tents of [c]Kedar! 6　　Too long has my soul had its dwelling 　　With those who [a]hate peace. 7　　I [a]am *for* peace, but when I speak, 　　They are [b]for war.	שִׁיר הַֽמַּעֲלוֹת אֶל־יְהוָה **Psa. 120:1** בַּצָּרָתָה לִּי קָרָאתִי וַיַּעֲנֵנִי ׃ יְהוָה 2 הַצִּילָה נַפְשִׁי מִשְּׂפַת־שֶׁקֶר מִלָּשׁוֹן רְמִיָּה ׃ 3 מַה־יִּתֵּן לְךָ וּמַה־יֹּסִיף לָךְ לָשׁוֹן רְמִיָּה ׃ 4 חִצֵּי גִבּוֹר שְׁנוּנִים עִם גַּחֲלֵי רְתָמִים ׃ 5 אֽוֹיָה־ לִי כִּי־גַרְתִּי מֶשֶׁךְ שָׁכַנְתִּי עִם־ אָהֳלֵי קֵדָר ׃ 6 רַבַּת שָׁכְנָה־לָּהּ נַפְשִׁי עִם שׂוֹנֵא שָׁלוֹם ׃ 7 אֲנִי־שָׁלוֹם וְכִי אֲדַבֵּר הֵמָּה לַמִּלְחָמָה ׃

References

Psalm 120:0
[†]Ex 34:24; 1 Kin 12:27

Psalm 120:1
[a]Ps 18:6; 66:14; 102:2; Jon 2:2

Psalm 120:2
[a]Ps 109:2; Prov 12:22
[b]Ps 52:4; Zeph 3:13

Psalm 120:3
[a]Ps 52:4; Zeph 3:13

Psalm 120:4
[a]Ps 45:5; Prov 25:18; Is 5:28
[b]Ps 140:10

Psalm 120:5
[a]Gen 10:2; 1 Chr 1:5; Ezek 27:13; 38:2, 3; 39:1
[b]Song 1:5
[c]Gen 25:13; Is 21:16; 60:7; Jer 2:10; 49:28; Ezek 27:21

Psalm 120:6
[a]Ps 35:20

Psalm 120:7
[a]Ps 109:4
[b]Ps 55:21

Targum

Psa. 120:1 A song that was uttered on the ascents of the abyss. In the presence of the LORD, when I was in distress, I prayed, and he received my prayer. **2** O LORD, deliver my soul from lips of deceit, from a deceptive tongue. **3** What does he give to you, O slanderer? And what does he add to you, O defamer, deceptive tongue? **4** The arrows of a warrior, sharp as lightning from above, with coals of broom that burn in Gehenna below. **5** Woe is me, for I have settled down with the oasis-dwellers; I have dwelt with the tents of the Arabs. **6** More than these, my soul abides with Edom, the hater of peace. **7** I am peaceful, for I will pray; [but] they are for war.

Spiritual Awareness

Introduction

The next fifteen psalms describe the rising fortunes of wise persons. They are called a Song of Ascents because the Children of Israel are worthy to ascend. They do not climb one rung at a time, but numerous rugs at a time. However, if Israel cannot follow the LORD, they will descend many levels as once (Deuteronomy 28:43). They sang these fifteen Psalms in the Temple because they believed that Israel's ascent would occur in that location.

Verse five

Meshech was a son of Japheth, son of Noah. Kedar was a son of Ishmael. These people were Bedouins. The Psalmist says that if evil overtook him, it would be equivalent to living like a Bedouin. These people did not have a permanent place to live. They moved from location to location in the desert. It is best to do good and live according to the words of the LORD. By living in this manner, one will have a permanent place to spiritually live. It also can refer to the next world. Upon death, a righteous person has better options than a sinful person.

O would that I had sojourned among Meshech, that I dwelt besides the tents of Kedar.

APPENDIX

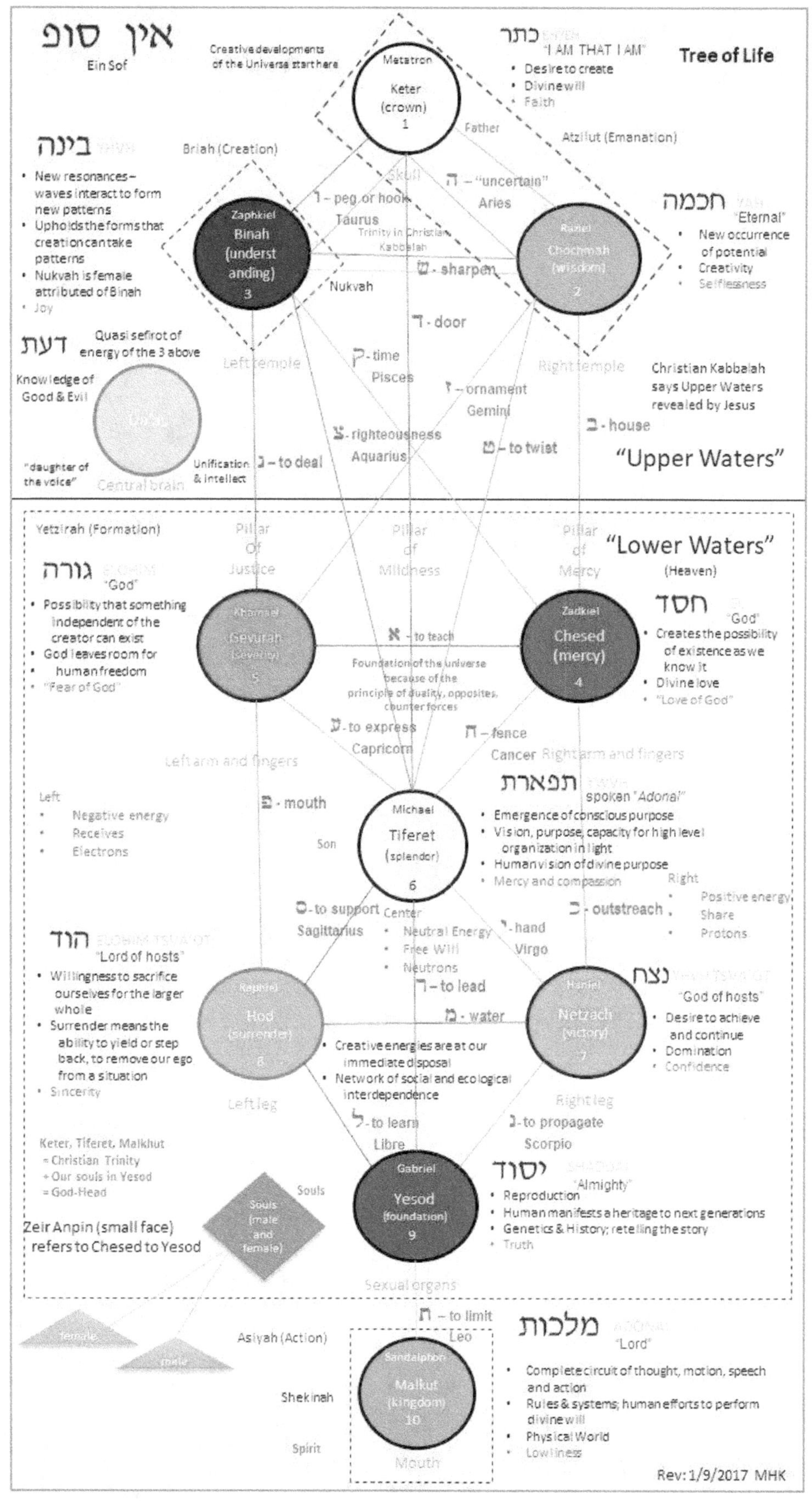
אין סוף
Ein Sof
Creative developments of the Universe start here
כתר
"I AM THAT I AM"
• Desire to create
• Divine will
• Faith
Tree of Life
Metatron
Keter (crown) 1
Father
Atzilut (Emanation)
בינה
• New resonances – waves interact to form new patterns
• Upholds the forms that creation can take patterns
• Nukvah is female attributed of Binah
• Joy
Briah (Creation)
Skull
ו – peg or hook
Taurus
Trinity in Christian Kabbalah
ה – "uncertain"
Aries
חכמה
"Eternal"
• New occurrence of potential
• Creativity
• Selflessness
Zaphkiel
Binah (understanding) 3
Raziel
Chochmah (wisdom) 2
ש – sharpen
Nukvah
ד - door
דעת
Quasi sefirot of energy of the 3 above
Knowledge of Good & Evil
"daughter of the voice"
ק – time
Pisces
ז – ornament
Gemini
בּ – house
Christian Kabbalah says Upper Waters revealed by Jesus
Da'at
Unification & Intellect
Central brain
צ – righteousness
Aquarius
כ – to deal
ט – to twist
"Upper Waters"
Yetzirah (Formation)
Pillar Of Justice
Pillar of Mildness
Pillar of Mercy
"Lower Waters"
(Heaven)
גורה
"God"
• Possibility that something independent of the creator can exist
• God leaves room for human freedom
• "Fear of God"
Khamael
Gevurah (severity) 5
א – to teach
Foundation of the universe because of the principle of duality, opposites, counter forces
Zadkiel
Chesed (mercy) 4
חסד
"God"
• Creates the possibility of existence as we know it
• Divine love
• "Love of God"
Left arm and fingers
Left
• Negative energy
• Receives
• Electrons
ע – to express
Capricorn
ח – fence
Cancer   Right arm and fingers
תפארת
spoken "Adonai"
• Emergence of conscious purpose
• Vision, purpose, capacity for high level organization in light
• Human vision of divine purpose
• Mercy and compassion
Michael
Tiferet (splendor) 6
Son
פ - mouth
Center
פ – to support
Sagittarius
• Neutral Energy
• Free Will
• Neutrons
י – hand
Virgo
ב - outreach
Right
Positive energy
Share
Protons
הוד
"Lord of hosts"
• Willingness to sacrifice ourselves for the larger whole
• Surrender means the ability to yield or step back, to remove our ego from a situation
• Sincerity
Raphael
Hod (surrender) 8
ר – to lead
ם - water
Haniel
Netzach (victory) 7
נצח
"God of hosts"
• Desire to achieve and continue
• Domination
• Confidence
Left leg
• Creative energies are at our immediate disposal
• Network of social and ecological interdependence
Right leg
Keter, Tiferet, Malkhut
= Christian Trinity
+ Our souls in Yesod
= God-Head
Zeir Anpin (small face) refers to Chesed to Yesod
ל – to learn
Libre
Souls
Souls (male and female)
Gabriel
Yesod (foundation) 9
נ – to propagate
Scorpio
יסוד
"Almighty"
• Reproduction
• Human manifests a heritage to next generations
• Genetics & History; retelling the story
• Truth
Sexual organs
female
male
Asiyah (Action)
Shekinah
Spirit
ת – to limit
Leo
Sandalphon
Malkut (kingdom) 10
Mouth
מלכות
"Lord"
• Complete circuit of thought, motion, speech and action
• Rules & systems; human efforts to perform divine will
• Physical World
• Lowliness
Rev: 1/9/2017 MHK

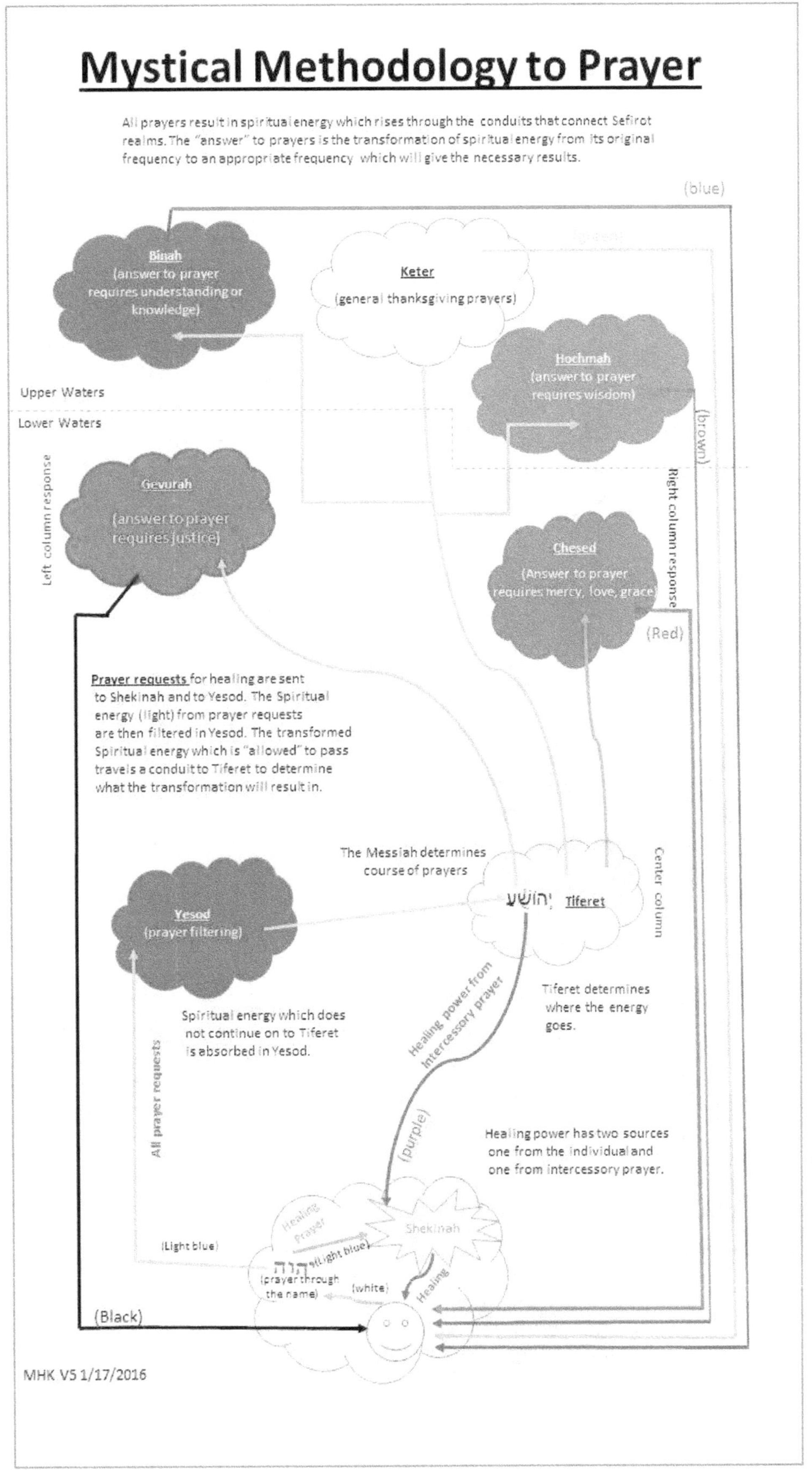

Mystical Methodology to Prayer
All prayers result in spiritual energy which rises through the conduits that connect Sefirot realms. The "answer" to prayers is the transformation of spiritual energy from its original frequency to an appropriate frequency which will give the necessary results.
(blue)
(green)
Binah
(answer to prayer requires understanding or knowledge)
Keter
(general thanksgiving prayers)
Hochmah
(answer to prayer requires wisdom)
(brown)
Upper Waters
Lower Waters
Left column response
Right column response
Gevurah
(answer to prayer requires justice)
Chesed
(Answer to prayer requires mercy, love, grace)
(Red)
Prayer requests for healing are sent to Shekinah and to Yesod. The Spiritual energy (light) from prayer requests are then filtered in Yesod. The transformed Spiritual energy which is "allowed" to pass travels a conduit to Tiferet to determine what the transformation will result in.
The Messiah determines course of prayers
יהושע Tiferet
Center column
Yesod
(prayer filtering)
Tiferet determines where the energy goes.
Spiritual energy which does not continue on to Tiferet is absorbed in Yesod.
Healing power from intercessory prayer
All prayer requests
(purple)
Healing power has two sources one from the individual and one from intercessory prayer.
(Light blue)
Healing Prayer
Shekinah
יהוה (light blue)
(prayer through the name)
(white)
Healing
(Black)

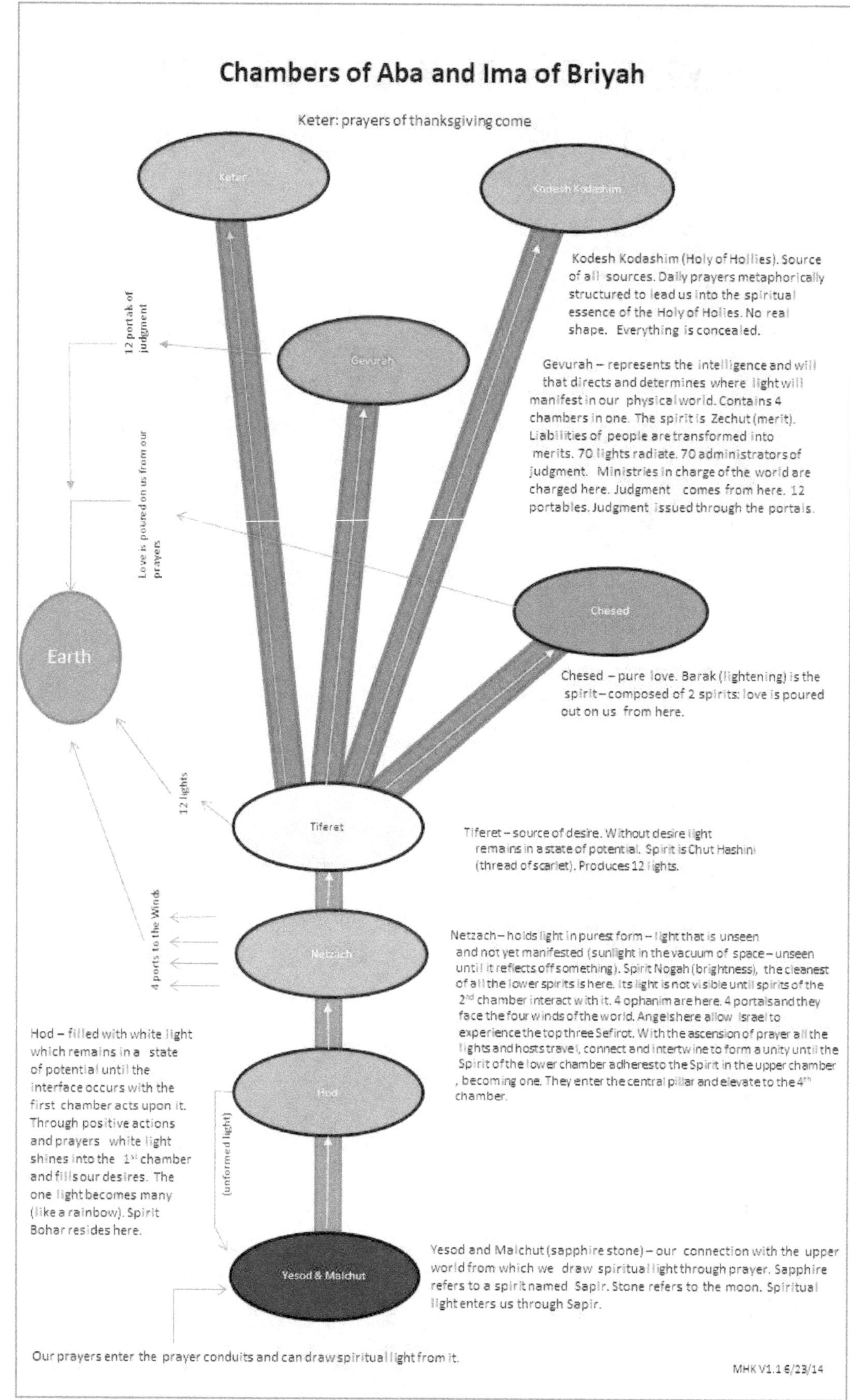
Chambers of Aba and Ima of Briyah

Keter: prayers of thanksgiving come

Keter

Kodesh Kodashim

Gevurah

12 portals of judgment

Love is poured on us from our prayers

Chesed

Earth

12 lights

Tiferet

4 ports to the Winds

Netzach

(unformed light)

Hod

Yesod & Malchut

Kodesh Kodashim (Holy of Hollies). Source of all sources. Daily prayers metaphorically structured to lead us into the spiritual essence of the Holy of Holies. No real shape. Everything is concealed.

Gevurah – represents the intelligence and will that directs and determines where light will manifest in our physical world. Contains 4 chambers in one. The spirit is Zechut (merit). Liabilities of people are transformed into merits. 70 lights radiate. 70 administrators of judgment. Ministries in charge of the world are charged here. Judgment comes from here. 12 portables. Judgment issued through the portals.

Chesed – pure love. Barak (lightening) is the spirit – composed of 2 spirits: love is poured out on us from here.

Tiferet – source of desire. Without desire light remains in a state of potential. Spirit is Chut Hashini (thread of scarlet). Produces 12 lights.

Netzach – holds light in purest form – light that is unseen and not yet manifested (sunlight in the vacuum of space – unseen until it reflects off something). Spirit Nogah (brightness), the cleanest of all the lower spirits is here. Its light is not visible until spirits of the 2nd chamber interact with it. 4 ophanim are here. 4 portals and they face the four winds of the world. Angels here allow Israel to experience the top three Sefirot. With the ascension of prayer all the lights and hosts travel, connect and intertwine to form a unity until the Spirit of the lower chamber adheres to the Spirit in the upper chamber, becoming one. They enter the central pillar and elevate to the 4th chamber.

Hod – filled with white light which remains in a state of potential until the interface occurs with the first chamber acts upon it. Through positive actions and prayers white light shines into the 1st chamber and fills our desires. The one light becomes many (like a rainbow). Spirit Bohar resides here.

Yesod and Malchut (sapphire stone) – our connection with the upper world from which we draw spiritual light through prayer. Sapphire refers to a spirit named Sapir. Stone refers to the moon. Spiritual light enters us through Sapir.

Our prayers enter the prayer conduits and can draw spiritual light from it.

MHK V1.1 6/23/14

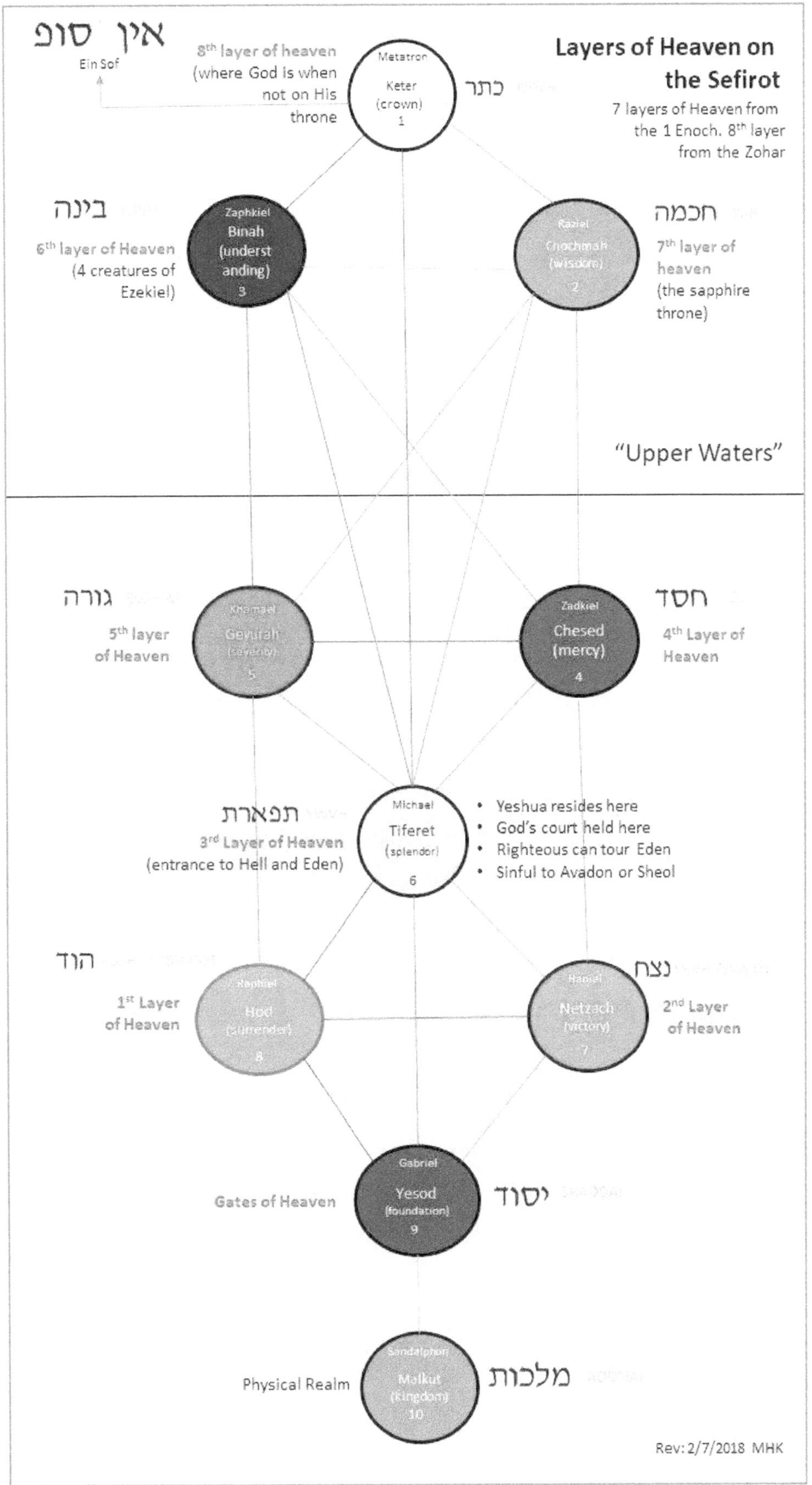
אין סוף
Ein Sof
8th layer of heaven (where God is when not on His throne)
Metatron
Keter (crown)
1
כתר
Layers of Heaven on the Sefirot
7 layers of Heaven from the 1 Enoch. 8th layer from the Zohar
בינה
6th layer of Heaven (4 creatures of Ezekiel)
Zaphkiel
Binah (understanding)
3
Raziel
Chochmah (wisdom)
2
חכמה
7th layer of heaven (the sapphire throne)
"Upper Waters"
גורה
5th layer of Heaven
Khamael
Gevurah (severity)
5
Zadkiel
Chesed (mercy)
4
חסד
4th Layer of Heaven
תפארת
3rd Layer of Heaven (entrance to Hell and Eden)
Michael
Tiferet (splendor)
6
• Yeshua resides here
• God's court held here
• Righteous can tour Eden
• Sinful to Avadon or Sheol
הוד
1st Layer of Heaven
Raphael
Hod (surrender)
8
Haniel
Netzach (victory)
7
נצח
2nd Layer of Heaven
Gabriel
Yesod (foundation)
9
יסוד
Gates of Heaven
Sandalphon
Malkut (kingdom)
10
מלכות
Physical Realm
Rev: 2/7/2018 MHK